Picnic Crumbs

A Gathering of Picnics,
Packed Lunches and Provisions
At Home and Abroad

Anabel Loyd

British Library Cataloguing in Publication Data.
A catalogue record for this book is available from the British Library.

ISBN 978-0-9570481-0-2

Published by
Polperro Heritage Press,
Clifton-upon-Teme, Worcestershire
WR6 6EN
United Kingdom
www.polperropress.co.uk

Printed in Great Britain by
Orphans Press, Leominster
United Kingdom

Contents

Foreword   5

Picnic Crumbs   9

Introduction   13

First Picnics   21

Equipment and Essentials   35

Boating Feasts and Follies   47

Picnics and Romance   63

Home, Work and Tradition   73

On Trains and Aeroplanes   87

Battles, Rations and Picnics in the Field   101

Abroad, and Travel Food   115

Agnes Jekyll, Hilda Leyel and other Cooks' Excursions   135

Social Graces and Summer Seasons   147

Provisions   161

Royal and Imperial   179

Disasters, Discomforts and Emergency Rations   189

School Food   207

A Finale of Sandwiches and Filling Stuff   219

En Fin   237

Bibliography   241

Foreword

Ah, the smell of it! Carcinogenic sausages being incinerated by Papa. Ah, the taste of it! Sand sandwiches with marmite and lettuce on the beach with Nanny. Ah, the grandeur of it! The sushi bars and cocktail mixologists in marquees now to be found at the ultimate picnic with bankers at the Fourth of June at Eton.

I am delighted that Anabel Loyd's enchanting and erudite treatise on picnic heaven has no truck with the latter. The perfect picnic summons up everything delightful about the outdoors: sunburn, a blinding wind, discomfort and probably the dog being sick. This is why the picnic is indispensable to the idiosyncratic British psyche and was an Empire-building endeavour. When the Good Lord divided the loaves and the fishes I cannot imagine that He thought the divine result would be an eternal sardine sandwich. Anabel, while espousing the sardine con brio, really glows when she introduces us to the picnics of yore à la Edward VII at the opera. Glyndebourne, Garsington and the Grange picnic competitors please note lobster mayonnaise, plovers' eggs, lamb cutlets, Parisian pastries and that "Gold plate was taken along as well to remind the King that it was a royal meal, even if it came from hampers".

Queen Victoria seems to have been ruthless at demanding passing peasants to boil water for her kettle in their cottages, so she and John Brown could have a cuppa, but at least she plonked her little round self in the heather. King George V and Queen Mary sat on upright chairs on the shores of Loch Muick while a ghillie set forth in a rowing boat to net brown trout. Loelia, Duchess of Westminster, recalls that "We gathered up the sliver slithering fish in buckets and took them to the chef who, in full regalia, white cap and all, was ready with a hot fire." The fish fry was then served by footmen and 'Was delicious as anything that I have ever tasted".

We know that our own dear Queen favours the burnt sausage but surely one of the many regrettable aspects of the decommissioning of the Royal Yacht *Britannia* is the loss of the picnic equipment list. During Her Majesty's summer cruise the boatswain was responsible for the landing arrangements for picnics with the appropriate equipment which included two tents, ground sheets, a shovel, gas lamps, blankets and 'Games (buckets, spades, balls)'. One feels rather more warmly towards Princess Margaret after discovering that her trips to the ballet or theatre would be followed by picnicky dinners: 'a cold chicken with lovely salads' or a 'picnic with steaks', details Anabel unearthed from Leo Groden's *My Royal Cookbook*.

Indeed, her research has been formidable. For most of us our acquaintance with Elizabeth David consists of *An Omelette and a Glass of Wine* but Anabel has dug deep to find David's description of the Maharajah of Jaipur's picnic in 1937 consisting of cold curry of boar's head (without the eyes) and a hamper of whisky.

I certainly can never resist the allure of P.G. Wodehouse and Anabel recalls young Bingo's paean to a picnic in *Jeeves and the Old School Chum:* "There's ham sandwiches," he proceeded, a strange, soft light in his eyes, 'and tongue sandwiches and potted meat sandwiches and game sandwiches and hard-boiled eggs and lobster and a cold chicken and sardines and a cake and a couple of bottles of Bollinger and some old brandy." "It has the right ring," Bertie said "And if we want a bite to eat after that, of course we can go to the pub."

Foreword

Picnic Crumbs is sprinkled with charming recipes – Coronation Chicken, Bloody Mary, Asparagus Rolls – that are balm to the soul, although I might pass on the udder sandwich. My personal picnic innovation is the wide-necked thermos – perfect for keeping new potatoes hot, buttery and minty to be eaten with Alderton ham marinaded in marmalade by Richard Craven-Smith-Milnes (available by post from Country Victuallers). What Anabel Loyd has achieved, with subtlety and gentle humour, is a chronicle of food fashion with a bracing whiff of the great outdoors. As the modern picnic sadly owes more to M&S, Prêt and the disposable barbecue than to Mrs David or Nanny, mistress of the egg sandwich, who does not long for curried boar's head?

Victoria Mather
London, May 2012

Picnic Crumbs

A Gathering of Picnics, Packed Lunches and Provisions at Home and Abroad

'I can recall in vivid detail the sense of freedom, the anticipation of meals that would be different, the feeling of summer heat as I stretched on the grass. Never has the whirr of a mowing-machine been so suggestive of holiday freedom. Going away for a youngster can be a crescendo of pleasures. They merge in a succession of joys. There is an unconscious retransfiguration of things both trite and commonplace. Somehow I always associate such reactions with picnic days. Picnic baskets have a spell of their own. Hard-boiled eggs are hardly a delicacy, yet they taste differently when eaten in the open air, particularly when the salt is produced in a screw of newspaper. Nobody wishes to devour sandwiches for ever, but it is remarkable how delectable two smeary pieces of bread encasing unappetizing cold beef can become. The meal has almost sacramental significance. As a connoisseur once remarked, the essential quality of a picnic is the doing of perfectly normal things in an abnormal place or manner. It is that quality that appeals so strongly to youth, the mental picture of adults squatting in a circle round baskets and glasses and bottles.'

(Louis T. Stanley, *The London Season*)

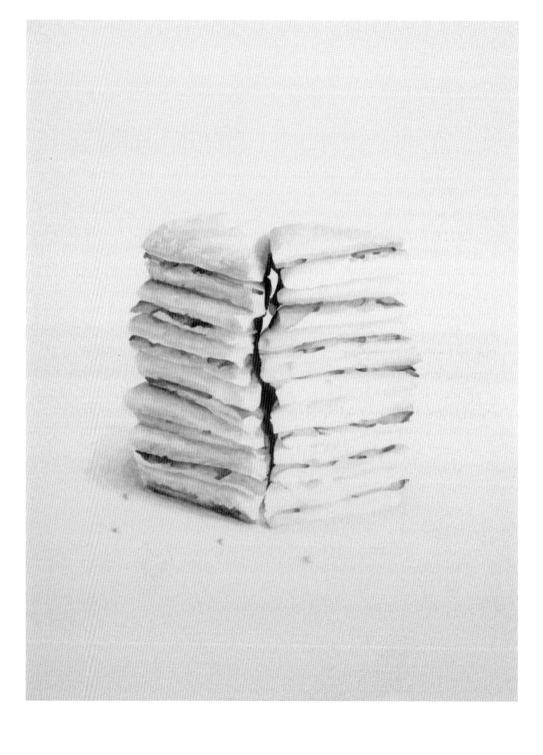

This book is for friends and family and especially for Heather, who taught me to make mayonnaise and made unsurpassable picnics; for Bobs, who took food very seriously, and for Mrs Macneil, who first allowed me to mess about in her kitchen.

I was inspired by two people who drew my attention to a contemporary gap in what I had thought to be an already crowded market. The first, a friend of my youngest daughter, eating her way through the home-made minced duck samosas, products of rather mixed Asian ancestry, that were part of a parents' day picnic last year, said: 'These are absolutely delicious, where did you get them?' The other, my eldest daughter's boyfriend, the artist Peter Haslam Fox, suggested a picnic book on the basis of my austerity family Christmas present, a small miscellany of Christmas snippets à la John Julius Norwich's *Christmas Cracker* and called 'Pudding Crumbs'. Fox thought that 'Picnic Crumbs' should be the next step and this latest effort is greatly improved by his whimsical and wonderful illustrations.

Introduction

'"The war is no picnic", someone will remark from time to time, and that phrase alone proves how high a place the picnic holds in man's affection. It offers through the generations a quiet and rustic ideal, attainable only during spells of utter calm, snatched from the world's restlessness and disillusion. Indeed a picnic resembles an essay in that its whole purpose is to afford pleasure; and it therefore seems appropriate that an essay, or part of one, should be dedicated to it ... Yet nobody I think, would pretend that it was other than an ugly word, picnic, verging on chit-chat or snip-snap ... It is, in fact, a busy, self-assertive, mediocre word that has sacrificed all dignity, but without attaining any compensatory sense of ease. Imagine the loss to us had Manet, for example, name his famous picture *Le Pique-Nique* instead of *Déjeuner sur l'Herbe*. Again, to eat *al fresco* sounds much more delightful than to picnic – but then it does not possess quite the same significance; to eat out-of-doors is not enough, otherwise the every snack of every tramp would constitute a picnic ... No, it implies – though this shade of meaning is contained in no definition of the word to be found in a dictionary – that one has a home and eats out-of-doors by choice.'

(Osbert Sitwell, *Picnics and Pavilions*)

Introduction

A book of picnics and picnic food is nothing new. There are manuals, the 'essential picnic recipes' with lists of foods for every outdoor occasion; volumes on picnics in art and literature, glossy with photographs and spiked with visually delicious recipes; chapters of information on intelligent picnic baskets and inspiring locations. The doyennes of cookery writing, Constance Spry, Elizabeth David, Claudia Roden, and others less widely known to casual cooks today, have beguiled their readers for a century or more with stories of picnics, their own and other people's, whetting appetites for outdoor eating, picnics and picnic foods from around the world. Using reminiscence as much as recipes they have created a sense of time and place, of convivial scenes, sunlight and unhurried pleasures to be treasured among other memories of busy lives. Their descriptions are punctuated with perfect recipes and the fruits of scholarly investigation into other and earlier food writers and those whom circumstances force to eat outdoors as well as true lovers of alfresco entertainments.

Picnic Crumbs too is a tally of memories, mostly other people's and occasionally my own. It revisits the work of innumerable food writers and descriptions of food and eating in less kitchen-orientated books and accounts that fit into the broad picnic category and somewhat, occasionally quite far, beyond. The selection is based on nothing at all beyond my enjoyment of a scene or the possibilities of the food conjured by the written description. My picnic memories range from the warmth of an Indian evening to a miraculously perfect summer interval at Glyndebourne or even scarcer days on the Scottish West Coast, where, from the rocks overlooking a white sand beach, a view of purple hills and glittering water to break your heart, make it the only place in the world to be. More typical is the squashed car interior in a wet car park waiting for some soggy school event when a good ham sandwich provides some small solace and may bring a greater optimism to lighten a dreary afternoon.

The Oxford Companion to Food summarises a broad selection of unsurprisingly unvarying definitions of the word 'picnic', mandatory to the introduction of any book on the subject. Preceded in the *Companion* by the mundane pickling onion, picnic is succeeded by piddock, an eatable of inspiring properties, capable of rendering luminous milk in which it is immersed, or breath if one is held in the mouth. Picnics can be as ordinary as the pickling onion or as magical as the luminescent piddock, a bacon sandwich on a suburban train or a perfect bento box, flower-viewing food, to be eaten as a pikunikku under the great cherry blossom canopies of the Japanese spring.

The late Alan Davidson, author of the *Companion*, writes: 'For many people, contemporary picnics involve an element of simplicity, where uncomplicated food such as hard-boiled eggs, sandwiches, pieces of cold chicken are eaten without ceremony.' True enough and this book has its fair share of hard-boiled eggs and sandwiches in humble settings besides more exotic and quixotic dishes eaten in less obvious situations.

Literary picnics and alfresco eating, whether fiction or fact, are inescapable, although the best known, such as Ratty's, do escape reiteration in these pages. Painted picnics appeal to the eye but there are difficulties in the successful identification of painted food that is only a small part of the composition or merely the titular excuse for a charming scene. Even at Tissot's beautifully painted picnics it hardly matters whether the cake is currant or sultana or the pie pork or game, the picnickers themselves are the point and likewise at a Brueghel peasant feast. I do, however, have an inherited painting of an Edwardian croquet game, with tea on the lawn, where the biscuits in the foreground are quite clearly Rich Tea; possible, as they were developed in Yorkshire as early as the 17th century.

Certain regional foods of the world are particularly transportable or otherwise suited to outdoor eating. Claudia Roden cites the dips, salads, filo pastries and pockets of Arab bread of the Middle East, as well as typical barbecues and whole roast lambs. In England an occasional hog roast will feed a whole community; Europe in late summer provides a constant feast of ripening grapes, figs and olives, with slices of garlicky, meaty salami in Italy; pizza bianca, hot from a village bakery; lasagne eaten from a cardboard dish sitting on Florentine steps, or a rough chunk of gritty parmesan with an apple, crunched between churches when sightseeing. In Spain, slices of jamón ibérico or manchego cheese with cubes of membrillo in the shade of a cork oak and in France the vast range of possible choices from a local market, *traiteur*, or even the stupendous supermarket where everything looks so much more desirable than at home.

In California the wealth of fruits and salads on show mean a picnic of free tastings before reaching the check out in a Napa Valley grocery store, or paying for a crowd-sized sandwich built at the deli counter of a Whole Foods supermarket in San Francisco. In Brazil a barbecue includes skewers of chicken hearts; quantities of meat top the bill for outdoor eating all over South America, supported by oceans of beans, bright salads and ubiquitous multicoloured corn on the cob. In South East Asia street eating starts at 5am in the markets of capital cities or small towns, with spicy dumplings, beef soup or chilli noodles, and Vietnamese street stalls sell instant picnics of fresh baguettes to eat with little pâtés wrapped in banana leaves.

Far to the North, whole salted herrings can be bought from hand carts in Dutch streets for eating on the spot; in Germany and Scandinavia, fat sausages with bread and a smear of strong mustard. In the Romanian Danube delta, a fisherman makes a *ciorba*, a fish soup of pike and catfish boiled outdoors over a fire, with vegetables and seasoning and in the Bulgarian mountain countryside where picnicking is popular, another soup, *kurban*, a meat stock coloured with peppers and tomatoes, is a traditional reminder of ancient animal sacrifices (Michael and Frances Field, *A Quintet of Cuisines*). Charcoal grilled corn on the cob is as much a staple street food in Eastern Europe as in South America or Africa where evening sales to hurrying pedestrians provide local women with a tiny income from surplus produce.

The nomadic peoples of Africa and Asia have nothing to learn about outdoor cooking and provisions, whether occasional feasts of meat and grains or the bare necessities for sustenance, a handful of dates in the desert; parched grain or *tsampa* in Tibet; the on the hoof meat larder of the Mongol herders, their long gone conquering hordes travelling ultra light, sustained mainly by drinking their horses' blood; the Masai and Nuer tribes, whose cattle provide their staples of milk and blood and only rarely meat. According to Reay Tannahill in *Food in History*, blood drinking or eating, has been common among pastoral peoples throughout history, the Arabs being particularly fond of a dish of mixed blood and camel hair and the Irish of a dish of blood boiled with milk, butter and herbs.

In the cities of North Africa and Turkey street sellers hawk their wares to peckish passersby and the streets are redolent of almond macaroons, oranges, frying doughnuts, sesame crusted bread and coffee. The Chinese are not obvious picnickers; one thinks instead of great formal dinners of perfectly balanced and presented courses, whether in the Forbidden City or the Great Hall of the People, but street stalls laden with soups, dumplings and orange coloured poultry offal offer scope for almost constant eating on the hoof. The focus of most Chinese festivals is on home and family and ancestral spirits need propitiation, their graves tended and their putative needs catered for; the Qingming Festival provides the best excuse for a family picnic in Chinese communities, when whole families and clans gather to sweep ancestors' graves and make offerings of wine and food to the dead followed by a grand graveside feast for the living.

The Victorians and Edwardians, at home and abroad may, aside from our own memories of picnics enjoyable or otherwise, be the inveterate picnickers at the centre of a picnic scene in our mind's eye although the use of the word picnic, in itself a Johnny-come-lately term for centuries of outdoor eating and packaged food, predates them by at least a century or so. Gilles Ménage's 1750 edition of the *Dictionnaire du Etymologique de la Langue Françoise* suggests that 'piquenique' may be of Spanish origin, first appearing in a French translation in 1664, although the Spanish do not use the word in any translation today. The *OED* dates the English translation to a letter from Lord Chesterfield in 1748 describing a social gathering and picnic thereafter became an expression for a shared outdoor meal to which participants all brought a dish, a definition with which *Larousse* concurs.

Introduction

Paying due deference to Victorian empire builders as indefatigable outdoor eaters wherever they were in the world, this book attempts, through the writings and memories of other feasters, fasters and travellers, to repeat tales that go beyond cold chicken and egg sandwiches in however many countries, to more unusual inventions, essentials and oddities of food and eating, carried, collected, prepared or eaten out of doors and away from formal kitchens, dining rooms and halls. In the end, it hardly matters what we call our outdoor feasts although there is no doubt, as Osbert Sitwell points out, that picnic is not a pretty word and there is no doubt that some of the descriptions of outdoor eating included in this book were, like war, no picnic at all.

First Picnics

If we begin only with the first use of the term picnic in whichever century or language it may first have been coined, we would lose an entire history of outdoor eating of one sort or another. A recent book on picnics opens with a group of 8th century monks seated on the ground to eat their meagre and carefully eked out supplies of cheese and salted horse head. They were wandering the famine stricken country with the miraculous relics of St Cuthbert after the sacking of Lindisfarne by the Vikings. It doesn't sound like much of a picnic (Jane Pettigrew quoting Reginald of Durham, *The Picnic*). Until the Romantic Movement transformed nature into art for those with the leisure and wealth to afford it, eating outdoors was more necessity than treat. Whether for conquerors and kings, religious or peasants, cooking and eating in the open were parts of everyday life, as they remain in parts of the world today. The concept of alfresco eating as entertainment is an 18th century invention, excepting perhaps at temples and churches on festivals and holy days, or when ancestral tombs were the sites of family gatherings and outdoor feasts that included both the living and the dead.

The best chronicled, if variably enumerated, mass outdoor meal of early modern history is well known. Whatever the size of the crowd, the actual numbers of loaves and fishes and whether or however they were miraculously multiplied, we assume that this was impromptu alfresco catering on a large scale.

From *Matthew, Chapter 15*:

> And Jesus saith unto them, How many loaves have ye? And they said, Seven, and a few little fishes.
>
> And he commanded the multitude to sit down on the ground.
>
> And he took the seven loaves and the fishes, and gave thanks, and brake them, and gave to his disciples, and the disciples to the multitude.
>
> And they did all eat, and were filled: and they took up of the broken meat that was left seven baskets full.
>
> And they that did eat were four thousand men, beside women and children.

Tinned kosher sardines from the Sea of Galilee can be bought on the internet. Their ancestors are the most likely candidates for the 'two small fishes' that, according to Matthew, Mark and John, with a loaves, barley or otherwise, fed the four, five, or even twelve thousand, not including unrecorded numbers of women and children. Morning caught sardines are at their best grilled outdoors on some southern beach where their smell is irresistibly inviting and a squeeze of lemon, bread and salt is all that is needed for a perfect lunch. However fresh, they never taste quite the same indoors in a restaurant.

Tinned sardines loom large in English food; in the nursery; on toast, as a savoury in old-fashioned clubs and dining rooms; or as the easiest and least large-boned of the endless smoked fish pâté starters of cut price 1970s dinner parties. Elizabeth David wrote a typically well researched article, *Oules of Sardines*, in 1962, that raised the profile of a humble little fish into, at its best a product 'of some delicacy, a treat rather than an everyday commodity'. In her day the French were, unsurprisingly, convinced of the pre-eminence of their sardines, fried in olive oil, over all others (*An Omelette and a Glass of Wine*). For French Foreign Legionnaires in Algeria in the 1960s, fighting on their stomachs meant lunches of bread, a tin of sardines and a raw onion eaten like an apple, washed down with a litre of rough wine.

Marika Hanbury Tenison, cookery editor of the *Sunday Telegraph* throughout the 1970s and wife of the explorer Robin, wrote in an article titled *First Catch Your Crocodile* that there were two 'basic requirements' for travelling with him, a tin of sardines and 'a large supply of celery salt, because jungle food is so tasteless...' The crocodile was 'really filthy' but the 'large red ants, fried to a crisp' were quite a successful addition to the essential sardines when dipped in the celery salt.

As children, sardine sandwiches were a teatime staple indoors and out, for tea on the lawn or the beach. In nursery days, while traditional battles waxed between nursery and kitchen, we ate what Nanny liked and by and large, excluding soft roes for breakfast, we liked what Nanny did. Her penchant for savoury over sweet resulted in shared picnics where our Marmite and lettuce, ham, or fishy sandwiches were occasionally unfavourably compared with our cousins' enviably sticky packages of sliced white bread filled with startlingly red jam. Our sardines were mashed into a rough paste with a little butter, not much less sophisticated than so-called sardine pâté and spread thinly on the strangely elongated rectangles of sliced white Scottish Mother's Pride. The delicious brown bread made in the kitchen by Mrs MacNeil in old Cow & Gate milk tins was not apparently considered suitable for sandwich making.

Brown bread in a milk tin

- 1 lb half plain, half wheaten flour
- 1 teaspoon baking soda
- 1 teaspoon Cream of Tartar
- 1 teaspoon salt
- 1 dessertspoon syrup
- Walnut-sized piece of butter

Mix altogether and add milk to make dropping consistency. Put into milk tin with lid and bake 1hr in moderate oven.

Mrs MacNeil cooked for us at our home on the Scottish West Coast island of Islay. I was only a few months old on my first visit and those early years of holidays and endless days with Nanny and my brother on a scrap of sand and rock, have blended into an undated memory of the gilded years of a peaceful and privileged childhood. I ate my first picnics on Islay and many more since, under the best or worst conditions. West Coast weather is not to be relied on; it can rain dismally for weeks on Islay or be transformed by days of bright sun, the hills and water shining in tweed colours making it the most beautiful place in the world.

As children we were dropped every morning at the beach with our buckets and spades and a good deal of Nanny's luggage. Mr MacNeil drove us down in the ancient, carefully nurtured LandRover, reappearing at lunch time with our picnic. If the rain came suddenly, gusting across the loch in grey sheets, we were reliant on him to drive back to the rescue, as we sheltered unsuccessfully in the lee of the rocks or paddled on happily, soaked to the skin, in the chilly rain-pocked shallows.

The best picnics were on Sundays when Mr and Mrs MacNeil took us on their day off expeditions to mysterious parts of the island and unfamiliar beaches. West Coast Scots, like their Irish near neighbours, have a taste for the macabre. Days out might include the graveyard and the ugly granite memorial, complete with ceramic photo plaque, to a recently dead baby, whose family was picked over like a chicken bone and whose image haunted me for weeks. The picnic itself was the high spot. Mrs MacNeil produced unexpected departures from our daily sandwiches and fruit; a flask of soup in addition to Nanny's usual tea; lamb rissoles or pieces of cold chicken; Mr MacNeil's tiny, matchless tomatoes, usually filched by us from the old conservatory attached to the house; an apple tart; buttered scones; or cakes of Mrs MacNeil's recent invention, the latest prize winners at the Womens' Institute, where she was the champion on an island full of good bakers.

When I was married in Wiltshire, Mrs MacNeil came south for the wedding and gave me as a wedding present a handwritten book of her recipes. None of them is very difficult or very exact. Their taste relies on good, fresh ingredients and, in the case of the apple tart, a lighter hand than I possess with pastry.

Creamy Carrot Soup

Coarsely grate 8oz carrots, 1 medium sized onion and a large potato; fry gently in 1oz of butter for 5 minutes, do not allow to brown.

Add ¾ pint of water and ¼ pint of milk; 1oz well-washed rice, a pinch of grated nutmeg, salt; bring to the boil, cover pan, lower heat and simmer very gently for ¾ - 1 hour.

Stir in 2 teaspoons lemon juice and 2-3 tablespoons fresh single cream. Reheat without boiling and sprinkle with chopped parsley before serving.

Apple Tart

For the short crust pastry: 6oz plain flour, 1¼ oz castor
sugar, 3¼ oz block margarine (Stork)
Cream margarine and sugar in Kenwood mixer; add flour
in tablespoonfuls and mix till well blended; knead on
floured board till smooth and free from cracks.
Line pyrex plate with pastry (a tin plate will do, not a pie
dish); dust lightly with cornflour to keep juice from soaking
into pastry. Stew apples and when cold put onto pastry
and cover with pastry lid. Prick all over with fork; make
a slit in centre to let stead escape and decorate edges.
Bake ¾ - 1 hour in slow oven until pale brown.

It doesn't sound very exciting now, when children eat the same food as their parents and anticipate multi-national picnic menus that reflect both their well travelled palates and the shelves of the local supermarket. Unsophisticated country-bred sixties children lived lives much closer to the wartime childhoods of their parents' generation than to that of the last decades of the 20th century. In Islay the corn was still stacked in old-fashioned stooks to dry; our vegetables came from the garden; our butter, milk and cream, in large quantities, from the farm. Running around beaches in flowery pants and hateful itchy fairisle jerseys, the height of our cosmopolitan ambition was reached with German cocktail sausages eaten straight from their little jars of brine.

We were sent to Scotland from our home in the South of England at the beginning of the summer holidays. Oh the excitement of the night train from Euston to Glasgow Central station and breakfast in the Central Hotel, starting with tomato juice, then porridge, eggs, kippers, toast and tea. On another train to the port of Gouroch, we caught our first delicious smell of the sea, then two successive ferries to Islay, with lunch in the white-clothed dining room on the second. Nanny suffered from travel sickness that necessitated the small and interesting medicinal flask of brandy in her handbag.

Our parents arrived later from warmer, more glamorous fortnights or so in the South of France or Italy. They brought housefuls of friends for a month or so of shooting, fishing, stalking and days of grown-up picnic lunches. My mother, who didn't much like Scotland or shooting, rebelled at the standard sponge-bagged shooting lunches of her in-laws' neighbouring estate. These rubbery packages were dished out indiscriminately and democratically to guests including prime ministers and other political luminaries and contained a bap filled with cold venison like a piece of shoe sole and a slice of tomato. Fillings were sometimes varied with ham, beef, mutton, or a piece of breakfast bacon and cold scrambled egg, with a bottle of beer to wash things down; an opener was attached with string to every bag. There would be two shattered water biscuits or cream crackers, glued together with a slab of Islay cheese; a piece of cake or chocolate and perhaps an apple.

The cheese, a mild cheddar type, was made until very recently in the Islay Creamery. It was called Dunlop after the village in Ayrshire where it was originally manufactured by Barbara Gilmour from the milk of Ayrshire cattle and is regarded as the national cheese of Scotland (F. Marian McNeill, *The Scots Kitchen*).

My grandfather and his friends, many of them politicians like the then Sir Alec Douglas-Home, were all brought up on the same sort of food, the fruits of family estates cooked in old fashioned kitchens by old fashioned Scottish cooks, whose gifts were mainly in baking and breakfast. The packed lunches eaten sitting in the heather would not have invited comment, adverse or otherwise, during conversations about the day, the grouse and possibly the latest news from London. More meritocratic political guests like Ted Heath, a serious gourmet who did not enjoy shooting or probably relish the adult version of nursery food enjoyed by many of his contemporaries at home and in their clubs, must have had a depressing time at lunch in the dining room. The food cooked by old Katie was redeemed mainly by her unequalled ginger bread at tea time.

Mrs Thatcher, a later arrival and a guest not altogether to my grandmother's taste (because the legend is true, she never went to bed), may have gone on picnics, I don't remember. She certainly continued to wear high-heeled shoes although was, I believe, persuaded into borrowed gumboots on occasional occasions. One imagines that considerations of food, good, bad, packed or on royal gold-plate were never allowed to dent her armour plating.

The last Prime Minister in waiting to appear on an Islay beach so far as I know (David Cameron spends time on the next door island of Jura) was Tony Blair. He knows about Scotland of course and arrived with his family from their regular holiday sojourn with friends on the mainland suitably clad in a thick jersey, sensible boots and the denim mufti of the Cool Britannia politician. They were excellent and enthusiastic picnic guests, politely consuming less than thrilling tuna mayonnaise baps by a grey sea in the usual howling gale and providing a good deal of excellent red wine that improved the climate no end.

According to Claudia Roden, the late Sir Ian Mactaggart, also an Islay landlord, described a 'popular lunch when stalking deer' as fried egg and bacon sandwiches in toast thick enough to survive the exigencies of a crawl. Those cold slabs of toast sound thoroughly unappetising but a bap or sandwich (untoasted) in the pocket remains the standard lunch when stalking on Islay although my family are far more demanding of individually crafted contents.

Agnes Jekyll writes about shooting luncheons when 'the hardy sportsman would make his frugal luncheon from the remains of the ample breakfast table, filling a roll with strange combinations of "left-overs" (as our American friends neatly call them), wrapping up a buttered scone with a slice of ham and a hard-boiled egg, adding a biscuit and a wedge of cheese, or perhaps only a piece of cake and an apple bulging his ample pockets'. She believes herself that 'the precious gifts of fresh air and exercise', should not be 'neutralized by over-elaborate feasting.' 'Good but simple' should be the keynote.

For a while, when she took charge, my mother decreed a new regime of hot lunches to be brought out to the shooters in Thermoses like insulated tiffin carriers and logistically possible due to the vicinity of drivable roads and tracks crisscrossing my father's land. I have never thought that boiled carrots and cauliflower went well with the outdoors or looked other than sad after an hour or two's warm incarceration in a sealed container. On the other hand, a good beef or lamb stew eaten with a spoon is not a bad thing when followed by a hunk of Dunlop cheese and the Terry's bitter chocolate that we only ever ate in Scotland. It came in dull gold and brown cardboard packets and snapped briskly into its large thin squares. In those early days before prep school and Mars bars, I don't think that milk chocolate had ever passed my lips. Our other sweets were boiled and came out of Nanny's pocket in a paper bag that she called a 'poke' in homage to her North of England background. Fudge and old-fashioned window pane toffee were made on the Baby Belling in the nursery.

This is the recipe for gundy, 'An old-fashioned sweetmeat' from the collection of traditional recipes gathered by F. Marian McNeill for *The Scots Kitchen* published in 1929.

Gundy

Pour into a saucepan a pound of brown sugar, a teaspoonful of syrup or treacle, and two ounces of butter.

Boil to the crack, that is, till it becomes quite hard when a little is put into cold water. Flavour with aniseed or cinnamon.

Pour out very thinly on a buttered tin or slab, and when it is cold and hard break up roughly with a small hammer; or when cool enough to handle form into thin round sticks.

Lady Jekyll's suggestions for hot shooting lunches are rather more precise, and whatever she believed, much more elaborate:

> 'A big brown marmite, piping hot from a hay-box, the contents fresh neck of mutton or lamb, with potatoes and small pickling onions; or, alternatively, a hotpot of game or poultry with celery, peeled chestnuts, and a milky gravy, flavoured with Worcester sauce or mushrooms, together with a bowl of jacket potatoes and a casserole of baked Boston beans. Jam or spiced apple puffs, covered-in cheesecakes or mince-pies, with butter and lettuces or celery, and a tin of mixed plain biscuits hotted up and served up crisp in their tin home, and a sportsman cake should be included.'

And that's not all:

> 'A brass dish of apples and pears makes the perfect centre-piece, and to comfort the chilly, slip in perhaps a box of dry Chinese ginger or some peppermint creams.'

This should all be served on a French gingham cloth with matching napkins, decorated with autumn leaves or 'a gay basket, holding a bunch of spindleberry or butcher's broom'. Be sure to 'lock up the port till dinner-time, if good shooting be desired'. (Agnes Jekyll, *Kitchen Essays*)

According to George Pryke, a gamekeeper in Shropshire all his life, shooting lunches before World War I may not have been so conducive to good shooting later. 'The Guns used to go to one of the farms for lunch but the keepers and beaters always took their own. No one went home sober. The chauffeur was always sent to the local pub to refill the beaters' beer jars, and the Guns always had a crate of whisky – not just one bottle.' (Brian P. Martin, *Tales of the Old Gamekeepers*)

Major L in *Breakfasts, Luncheons and Ball Suppers*, gives a very familiar picture of the best and worst of shooting lunches:

> 'It should be a cheery enough repast, though, of course, some of the conditions of its success are beyond human control. Nothing can be more joyless than consuming damp sandwiches upon a dripping rock, with a howling wind to roll

up the storm-clouds over the Ben behind you. A situation of this sort subdues even a Scotch keeper's omnivorous capacity for remnants, and the dogs get a larger share than usual of the crumbs which fall from their master's table. Yet the lunch on the moor is the lunch of the highest possibilities, which only require for their realisation a fine day. A lunch amid the purple heather, with a cloudless sky overhead, and just a ruffle of mountain breeze to tone down the effect of the blazing sun, which enables you to appreciate the cool waters of the burn brattling down the hillside into the blue loch below – such a lunch knows no rival in this present vale of tears.'

The advent of the disposable barbecue has added to the variety of easy picnic food for Scottish family picnics and improved the lot of the fed up holiday cook. Whereas a proper barbecue needs coaxing to light and careful nurturing to turn the flames to glowing charcoal, these tin foil trays of charcoal can be lit in a force 8 gale and will cook a few sausages in minutes; real barbecues need real cleaning too. Raw meat can be chucked into a bag and the cook abnegate all further responsibility to those with a fire fetish. The meat for fast heating and cooking throwaways benefits from advance dousing with soy or Worcestershire sauce, pepper and garlic salt, although local Scottish lamb and fillet steaks melt like butter and are consumed in appalling quantities by the usual army of enormous, immensely hungry teenage boys.

Gifts of sides of smoked salmon or gravadlax from the Loch Fyne Smokery are welcome additions to the Scottish holiday larder and picnic. Digby Anderson, the *Spectator*'s Imperative Cook gives clear instructions, with diagrams, for the construction of a home smoker, a proper thing with a chamber and a chimney (*Imperative Food*). It all sounds a bit like hard work but making Gravadlax is easy as pie, cheap as chips and successful with salmon of most inferior provenance. Two sides sandwiched together under layers of dill, sugar and salt and weighted at the bottom of the fridge for a week will be good enough for the fussiest foodie. There is no great magic or skill required to whisk up mustard and dill sauce to go with it and dried dill works just fine. In Islay, a little way offshore, there is a small uninhabited island, reached by boat on calmer days, with the perfect flat coffin-shaped stone just above the beach, for carving cured sides of fish while barbecues are lit on the pebbles below.

Tinned sardines have disappeared from recent picnics in the face of such riches. Lately there have been oysters too, from an island farm using its location on the shores of a sea loch to diversify into oyster production. The oyster beds provide the nuttiest, freshest taste of the sea, and with an oyster knife, Tabasco and a lemon, an instant picnic in the adjacent dunes. The opposite shore of the loch is the place for huge lunch time gatherings of friends and extended family, 40 or more cousins and kinsmen, with ill-assorted packs of dogs, the best bred spaniels and the most mistakenly born mongrels in every size and shape. An excess of lobsters from the local lobster man means the remains of dinner as lobster mayonnaise, another luxury addition to ham or barbecued sausages of which Lady Jekyll would have approved. Lobster is unfortunately much to the taste of the 'dorgies', two badly mannered, low-slung and hairy sisters with royal connections and mixed ancestry for whom a plastic box with an ill-fitting lid is no obstacle to joint endeavour and intense greed.

Enough alcohol is essential to the multi-generational beach picnic, oiling old and arthritic appreciation of the young, ravenous and incredibly loud and encouraging healing post-prandial sleep for all ages. My husband's Bloody Mary recipe is straight from the Dean Martin school of cocktail making – for choice his vodka is lightly coloured with tomato juice. For more general use, he considers himself, after years of experimentation, to have the perfect formula, which is made and drunk in industrial quantities.

Bloody Mary

To one large bottle of Mott's Clamato Juice in a
jug add Worcestershire sauce, Tabasco sauce,
celery salt, a spoonful of grated horseradish,
ground black pepper, juice of half a lemon, ice
and vodka at a judicious level of 1-4, to be raised
according to need.

Give it all a good whisk/shake. To find the
optimum spice levels for individual taste requires
regular tasting and testing .

Although the Bloody Mary must have been invented in time at least for later PG Wodehouse Jeeves and Wooster stories, it doesn't crop up before or between the Bollinger and the brandy in the books – perhaps Wodehouse was not a fan of such concoctions. This picnic, however, encompasses many picnic favourites including some mentioned above and, with the carrots out and the Bollinger in, manages to sound perfectly delicious.

> '"I've just been supervising the packing of the lunch basket, Bertie," he said. "I stood over the butler and saw that there was no nonsense."
> "All pretty, sound?" I asked, relieved.
> "All indubitably sound."
> "No carrots?"
> "No carrots," said young Bingo. "There's ham sandwiches," he proceeded, a strange, soft light in his eyes, "and tongue sandwiches and potted meat sandwiches and game sandwiches and hard-boiled eggs and lobster and a cold chicken and sardines and a cake and a couple of bottles of Bollinger and some old brandy"
> "It has the right ring." I said. "And if we want a bite to eat after that, of course we can go to the pub."
>
> (PG Wodehouse, *Jeeves and the Old School Chum*)

Equipment and Essentials

'Preparing and serving outdoor meals has, like other phases of this
sort of housekeeping, a distinct technique. A thorough familiarity
with certain rules greatly simplifies one's problems and adds much
to the charm and pleasure of eating al fresco.'

(Elizabeth Case & Martha Wyman, *Cook Away - the outing cook
book*)

'We hold that a pic-nic is not a pic-nic where there are well-arranged
tables and powdered footmen to wait. It is merely an uncomfortable
out-of-door dinner. A pic-nic should entail a little of the trouble and
enterprise of life, gathering sticks, lighting the fire, boiling the pot, buying
or stealing the potatoes. It is an excellent training for housekeeping, and
affords a favourable opportunity for developing the skill of young ladies,
in an art, that as servants go, they all seem likely to have to come to sooner
or later, namely, waiting on themselves. Moreover, what one cooks oneself
is always much better than what anybody else cooks for one, just as the
money that a man makes is always a great deal more prized than what
comes jingling in of itself.

Our party on this occasion was of the well-supplied order — plenty of
everything, and plenty of servants to hand things about. Some brought
their butlers, because the butlers chose to come; some brought their
footmen to show their new liveries; some their pages to keep them out of
mischief. And though there were a few of the usual casualties of moving,
such as the salt coalescing with the sugar, and the pickles bursting into
the pie, the servants had the rectification of matters, and there was no
scrambling for plates, no begging for forks, no two people eating with one

spoon. All was orderly and orthodox, plenty of provisions with the usual preponderance of hams, tongues, and chickens.' (R. S. Surtees, *Plain or Ringlets*, quoted by Claudia Roden, *Picnics and other Outdoor Feasts*)

Jerome K. Jerome's description, for comic effect, of picnic equipment and essentials doesn't sound particularly extreme to the British picnic maker, even quite modest, especially compared with Surtees' fictional over-staffed affair.

> 'There seemed a good deal of luggage, when we put it all together. There was the Gladstone and the small hand-bag, and the two hampers, and a large roll of rugs, and some four or five overcoats and macintoshes, and a few umbrellas, and then there was a melon by itself in a bag, because it was too bulky to go in anywhere, and a couple of pounds of grapes in another bag, and a Japanese paper umbrella, and a frying pan, which, being too long to pack, we had wrapped round with brown paper.'   (*Three Men in a Boat*)

The grandest picnic cases came from Aspreys of Bond Street, with porcelain plates and silver fittings. Harrods and other emporiums made their own and, for the more charitable and economically inclined, the Lord Roberts Workshops for disabled service men produced large wicker hampers with any number of variations on the theme. Elizabeth David recommends older Edwardian picnic hampers which 'may be cumbersome, but they are capacious and solid; an aura of lavish gallivantings and ancient Rolls-Royces hangs about them'. I can't altogether agree unless you still have the Edwardian footman instead of the 21st century husband to lug them out to the Rolls and the scullery maid to clean up later   It seems, however, that grandeur and inconvenience still sells; plastic moulded cold boxes and 'eskis' are being discarded in cases of picnic one-upmanship for a huge variety of new fitted cases and hampers with names like Balmoral and Ascot and plenty of bone china plates and crystal glasses. Perhaps their users take a leaf out of Gertrude Jekyll's book and carry portable picnic decorations as well.

Well I'm afraid I'm just too idle – aside from the joys of on the spot cooking, requiring a barbecue or a fire of some sort, enough plates and cutlery to avoid burnt fingers and minimum advance food preparation; I would rather have good food in plastic boxes; if necessary on paper plates that can all be chucked in the rubbish; certainly nothing that needs worrying about or washing carefully by hand. A recent gift catalogue advertises a portable sink; wouldn't you just be thrilled if you found one of those in your Christmas stocking? F. Marian McNeill is very clear about the importance of washing up properly in a large camp where 'method is essential' and regimentation of the campers too it seems.

> 'Method is even more essential in the washing-up. There should be plenty of hot water in readiness, and immediately the meal is over, the dishes should be cleared and piled in readiness.
>
> It greatly facilitates matters if the cooks do their own washing-up, and the scullions theirs. The rest can be done by five or six workers in rotation, two washing, the others drying and putting away.
>
> The essential things are plenty of thoroughly hot water and dry towels, with soap powder, soda, or wood ash for saucepans or greasy dishes. (Do not, however, use soda for aluminium ware. It ruins it.)'

Mrs Beeton points out the importance of 'choosing congenial guests' to make 'a well-arranged picnic one of the pleasantest forms of entertainment' and cautions only against such mistakes as forgetting the corkscrew to open the 'abundance of wine'. These occur all too frequently without proper planning of a menu that adds 'all the little etceteras', but 'Paper plates and dishes will save both weight and room in the hamper, and can be burned after having been used'. Some food may taste better on porcelain plates but if it's good enough in the first place it will probably bear up to plastic. Eating fried rice from melting paper plates in monsoon rain in India was just one rare convenience step too far.

In this country people worry overmuch about cold food getting hot and freeze things to death with the weight of ice packs in the cold box. Drinks obviously need to be kept cold and hot soup, for instance, hot in a Thermos, but, for my taste, most food is better left at room temperature or to reach room or outdoor temperature once it is out of the fridge. Sandwiches are disgusting when icy cold as we must all know from the plastic and blotting paper horrors of motorway service stations.

A lot of food tastes at its best luke-warm. The most popular picnic food is sticky honey and mustard coated sausages, spiced chops or chicken pieces, wrapped in foil, newspaper and the old picnic rug and unpacked still warm. Plates – plastic probably; glasses, ditto; napkins; a cloth, maybe, and all the packeted biscuits, crisps, or whatever, are hurled into one of those huge striped Chinese bags, breakables on top if possible. All the packed up boxes, bowls and trays can go in whatever can be found to keep them the right way up and in one piece. It is vital to remember a bin bag for the rubbish and another for dirty hardware and, if things need to be carried far, it is rather important to have durable boxes, bags and baskets with decent handles.

Major L, author of *The Pytchley Book of Refined Cookery and Bills of Fare*, in his *1887 Breakfasts, Lunches and Ball Suppers,* written in the third person, defines his perfect Luncheon Basket, with a good deal of advice as to its contents.

> 'Luncheon baskets, as a rule, he considers badly designed; a large tin case with no divisions, one or two large bottles, which take up nearly all the room and assist in spoiling wine if decanted into them, three or four tumblers, and there you are – no room for what is really requisite; so he is conceited enough to think that a basket that he has designed, with the assistance of Messrs. Farrow & Jackson is a great improvement on any he has seen. It contains a dish in which a pie can be baked, a tin case with a division, in which cold poultry, game, or meat can be taken, on one side, and bread, cake, plum pudding, or pastry on the other; it is designed to hold two pint bottles, one for champagne or claret, the other for sherry or Salutaris water. Instead of two tumblers and two small glasses, which take up much room, it is fitted with two large and two small cups of transparent horn, fitting one inside the other, and

taking up the room of one tumbler only; they are exceedingly light, clean, and nice. It is, of course, fitted with pepper, salt, and mustard; knives, forks, two plates, and a portable table is fastened outside, which he considers is a great advantage, in fact an absolute necessity for comfort.'

Hunting Pies

Having obtained a baking tin the size of the hunting-case, or if carried in a pocket, a tin three inches square and three-quarters deep, line with pastry for meat pies not quite a quarter of an inch thick. Cut in squares, the size of dice, either the lean of fillet of beef, mutton, chicken and ham, veal and ham, grouse, hare, partridge, or pheasant; season mutton or beef with chopped parsley, and if not disliked, the slightest soupçon of chives or onion, and the other meats with sliced mushrooms or truffles, and the whole with pepper and salt; roll the meats in the seasoning and fill the tins, wet the top of the pastry in the tin and cover with pastry, leaving a small hole in the top; close the edges with a fork, and bake in a quick oven for fifty minutes. Let the pie get nearly cold, then take out of tin, and if the bottom and sides are not sufficiently baked, put in the oven until the pastry is cooked; take them out, and let them get nearly cold, when inject through the hole in the top some good meat jelly into the meat, and some aspic in the poultry and game pies. Let the pies get cold, and they are ready for use.

Like Major L, Colonel 'Wyvern' Kenney-Herbert served in India and has recommendations for the essential equipment for Camp Cookery in his

Culinary Jottings for Madras. These include the 'Acme stove', which sounds like a portable Aga with its cooking range and ability to heat a room or dry clothes. The 'Lang spirit lamp', is for lighter work and sudden cooking whim.

> 'I use mine for omelettes almost every day in cantonment, for which work it is admirably adapted. With a 'Lang lamp' you can make a cup of tea or coffee in the train, by the side of the road, on arrival at a public bungalow, or under a tree whist the lascars are pitching your tent; and by its aid, and that of a small frying pan, you can devil a biscuit, fry a rasher, poach an egg, or cook a kidney, to accompany the tea or coffee.'

The following recipe from *Culinary Jottings* sounds a good test of the Acme stove, not to mention the cook.

> 'Fresh-water fish is often to be had by men out in camp. Clean them thoroughly, wash them well to get rid of all muddy taste, scale, trim, and soak them after cleaning, in water. A fish like murrel may be treated like a pike: - after having been carefully cleansed and trimmed, stuff it with turkey forcemeat, sew it up, trim it in a circular shape with its tail in its mouth and bake it in a pie-sish surround by chicken stock about half an inch deep. A glass of any white wine like hock, chablis, or sauterne may be put into the stock, an onion also, and any vegetables you can spare. The fish should be basted every now and then, and when it has absorbed the gravy and seems soft, take it out of the oven. Put a pat of maître d'hôtel butter on the top of it, and serve in its own dish with a napkin folded round it. A good sized murrel will take from twenty minutes to half an hour in baking. A stuffing mad with a tin of oyster, well drained and cut up, mixed with a half pint of bread-crumbs soaked in milk or stock, some spiced pepper, a little chopped very finely pared lime peel, and a couple of minced anchovies, all stirred together, and bound with a couple of eggs, is highly acceptable with a murrel. If you have no oysters, pound a

good quantity of fresh-water shrimps, and mix them with the stuffing.'

'Wyvern' considered American camping equipment superior to British. For most travellers at home and abroad, the Army & Navy Stores provided, via its main store in London, or depots in Plymouth, Aldershot, Bombay and Calcutta. Lists and illustrations of goods ranging from wedding cakes like war memorials to canary seed, elephants' foot umbrella stands, corsets, cashmere and spare limbs, fill the pages of the massive 1907 mail order catalogue. In the vast range of comestibles suitable for explorers, adventurers and sportsmen from the tropics to the poles, many have well-known brand names; Heinz tomato ketchup; Tate & Lyle golden syrup; others, like the fraudulently advertised 'Eiffel Tower' lemonade crystals, are long gone.

There are luncheon baskets, tea baskets and the 'Lun-Tea' basket, the 'Train de Luxe' and 'The New Swing Kettle', not to mention, the 'Ever-Ready' tea or coffee case, the 'Sirram' 'En Pension' Tea Set' and 'The Infant's Travelling Companion' at 36 shillings. Besides 'strong chests for travelling', portable stoves, canteens and fittings, approved by the War Office for the use of infantry and cavalry officers; the camp dweller may use the Double-roof Ridge Tent, in 'green rot proof canvas', as supplied to the Congo State Government and Sir H. M. Stanley. He may sleep on the 'Improved X Compactum' camp bed or carry his house on his back as it were and use the "Mummery" Tent and Field Bivouac' weighing 9lb and looking frighteningly claustrophobic.

The civilised traveller will remove his cholera belt to bathe in his india-rubber bath, leaving his shoes on his shoe rack and his soiled linen in the correct bag. He will sip his whisky and soda while sitting on his Roorkhee Folding Chair, resting his copy of *Kim*, *Lord Jim*, a well thumbed *Rubaiyat of Omar Khayyam*, or the Bible if he feels the need, on his folding table, while waiting for his murrel to be stewed or his kidney cooked. He will have a portable washstand, shaving mirror, dressing cases, maybe a chest of drawers and a combined despatch case/writing desk, the 'Alliance'; with a gift from his mother, a silver pen wiper shaped like a pig. All being well he will also have plenty of porters.

It's all a bit different to Nanny on the beach with a packet of sardine sandwiches, a Thermos of tea and a hateful wet flannel in a sponge bag to clean fingers and faces. At least we didn't wear llama and silk combinations although we did have itchy wool vests and Nanny might very well have liked a 'Luxuriosum' bathing tent, striped, at 19 shillings and 9 pence, and so, I suppose, should we.

Claudia Roden has hard words for those modern travellers 'who spend far longer than they need painting and washing their yachts and fitting out their caravans' and then live on 'the ugliest products of industrialization and urbanization' instead of exploring suitable outdoor or local cooking methods and of course ingredients. She advocates cooking on the spot through whatever medium, improvised or the transported spirit lamp, is available. The one frying pan, cauldron or stewpot will provide at the very least a variation to the coldly depressing contents of yet another tin.

The Italians are good at outdoor food and travel with the necessities for its proper preparation. 'Walking through a pine forest along the sea front at Forte dei Marmi, we were amazed at the number of families sitting at tables eating spaghetti under the trees. Surrounded by chopping boards, sieves, frying pans and primus stoves, they had evidently prepared it on the spot and must have started early with the sauce. The Italians, I thought, cannot live without spaghetti.' (Claudia Roden, *Picnics and other Outdoor Feasts*)

Roden suggests another Italian dish, *fagioli al fiasco*; dried beans cooked with olive oil, garlic and sage in a large Chianti flask, minus its straw covering, in hot ashes for several hours. I am much addicted to one pot cookery and I like baked beans so long as they don't come out of a tin but, for similar time and trouble, old fashioned omnivorous one vessel meals sound more interesting. I imagine Major L would have had made the perfect cauldron for this sort of cooking over an open fire.

> 'Apparently as many as six or seven different foods were often cooked at one at one time by an ingenious method of co-ordination. Inside the giant pot, a flat plank of wood was wedged near the bottom, and under this a joint of meat – probably bacon or salt beef – was boiled, while on top of the board stood two or three earthenware jars, tightly sealed. Inside these might be found meat combined with root vegetables for soups and stew, eggs in the shell, and cut-up chickens. In a muslin bag hanging from the handles simmered either some dried vegetables or a boiled pudding.'

> (Arabella Boxer, *The Vogue Winter Cookbook*)

Arabella Boxer gives a recipe for a 'Bargee's dinner' that would once have been cooked on the tow-path over a fire.

Bargee's Dinner

Place a platform of sticks, or flat stones, in the bottom of a galvanised iron bucket. Half-fill it with water and bring to the boil over a bonfire or simple stove. Fill a large earthenware jar that has a lid with layers of lamb, cut in neat pieces with most of the fat removed, and a selection of vegetables cleaned and cut in large chunks; carrots, leeks, small whole onions, potatoes and turnips. Add salt and black pepper to each layer, and a handful of pearl barley, distributing it evenly throughout the layers, together with plenty of chopped parsley. Pour in enough water to fill the jar by about two-thirds. Make a thick paste of flour and water to seal the lid completely and tie a piece of cloth over the top. Place the jar in the bucket, and after the water regains boiling point, allow 2½-3 hours cooking time. Care must be taken to maintain a good heat, for the water must no go off the boil. A muslin bag, or even two, can be cooked in the pail at the same time. It could contain a pease pudding or haricot beans; these should be soaked beforehand, and will take about 1½ hours to cook, so should be added about 1 hour after the stew has started to cook.

Digby Anderson, Imperative Cook of the *Spectator* magazine is determinedly opinionated on what is and is not essential to a good picnic. He divides picnickers into the 'Fanatics', the 'Lazies' and, as always 'Chaps', people like him with a proper understanding of life, society and good food.

'Winter Picnics Fanatics spend half a day lading the car with calor gas stoves, tubular chairs and tables, barbecue assembly kits and reproduction Edwardian hampers. They have quantities of knives and plates and things but all are special picnic ones. For some curious reason, these are all children's size. Many are plastic or paper. One can always spot a Fanatic at Towcester by his typical contorted gesture as he struggles to keep a heavyweight commercial pork pie on a lightweight paper plate.

The Lazies, on the other hand, make a virtue of their laziness: 'We never plan it ahead, you know. If it looks a nice day, spur of the moment, I just say to Jean, "What about Towcester?" And we jump in the car and go. We can always pick up some bread and pâté en route.' They can't. They don't. The bread is sold out so they buy crisp fluffy rolls. The pâté shop is closed so they put up with plastic ham. Because they thought they were having pâté, they have no butter. If there is one thing it is almost impossible to swallow, it's an unlubricated British mass-produced crisp fluffy roll.

Chaps have lots of picnics so they know what is needed and there is no fuss. They take proper cutlery and crockery but no chairs or tables. In the country they sit on the grass: at the races they stand by the boot of the car from which they serve themselves and perch their plates either on the roof or the bonnet. Tablecloths are sometimes used in the country, spread on the grass. Car rugs are better. At the races neither are got out, however dirty the roof or the bonnet. But many Chaps like to take their napkins, in their rings. Paper towels are never used, partly because they are associated with the

Equipment-Fanatics who use cologne impregnated ones hoarded from their air-flights to Tenerife. Car rugs are good for wiping hands on.

Take plenty of cold roast birds; pheasants, partridges, chickens, a few teal or widgeon. But first perhaps some fish pâté, some turbot steaks with mayonnaise or artichoke hearts in oil. There should always be potatoes in their jackets. They are taken out of the oven just before departure and wrapped in old towels with some bottles of claret and put in the warmest place. By lunchtime they won't be very warm but the claret will be better than it would have been.'

The authors of *Cook Away* would approve a 'Chaps' picnic that 'necessitates considerable preparation ahead of time'. Their strictures for their five categories of successful alfresco eating exclude the claret but are clear on the importance of a good alcohol supply, especially in the camper van: 'Lack of space prevents much of a wine cellar but even the smallest of these temporary homes should have on hand Scotch, Bourbon or rye whisky, brandy and sherry for medicinal and culinary reasons if no other. Many will want to augment this minimum supply with gin, vermouth, both French and Italian, Angostura bitters and rum'. A fairly extensive driving drinks cupboard one would think, providing the makings of some useful medicinal cocktails; Manhattans; old-fashions mint juleps; and any number of Martinis.

Martini Cocktail No.1

3 parts gin

1 part combined ½ French vermouth/
½ Italian vermouth

Place in a shaker with ice. Stir well, don't
shake. An olive may be placed in each glass

Boating Feasts and Follies

'It is not the first object of your work to keep down expenditure, but it is your first duty to see a table of superior quality maintained on board your ship, and your passengers thoroughly well satisfied. It has seldom happened that a really good table was not an economical one, compared to one badly managed, but you must clearly understand that what we now instruct you to secure is first an excellent table, and secondly to combine your efforts in that direction with due economy; and it is the wish of the Directors that you should continually seek to improve the table arrangements on board your ship.'

(Memorandum for the Guidance of Pursers and Stewards-in-Charge on Victualling and Management, 1908, P & O Company.)
(Theodore Fitzgibbon, *The Pleasures of the Table*)

Gerald Durrell's descriptions of their life in pre World War II Corfu have fixed his idiosyncratic family, mother cooking endlessly for eccentric guests at its centre, in the imaginations of generations of his readers, and gilded Prospero's island with added magic. The story of Mother's birthday party from *Fillets of Plaice* begins with the accident-prone loading of the family's massive and far from portable ice box onto a *benzina* for a boat picnic on a grand scale and gives us one of the most memorable pictures of the family, their friends and their food.

'Then, eventually we reached the extraordinary brown and eroded coast between Albania and Corfu which spread on into Greece, and as we drew closer and closer to the coast we passed towering pinnacles of rock like the carunculated melted remains of a million multicoloured candles. Eventually, as night was falling, we discovered a bay that looked as though it had been bitten out of the hard rock by some gigantic sea monster. It was a perfect half moon, and here we thought we would make landfall. The sand was white, the cliffs tall and somehow protective, and so gently the benzina was brought in, the anchor was thrown over the side, and we came to a halt. This was the moment when the ice-box came into its own. Out of it Mother and Spiro unpacked an incredible assortment of foodstuffs: legs of lamb stuffed with garlic, lobsters, and various extraordinary things that Mother had made which she called curry puffs. Some of them were in fact curry puffs but others were stuffed with different delicacies. And so we lay around on the deck and gorged ourselves.

In the forequarters of the boat we had a great pile of watermelons that looked like an array of pudgy footballs, green with whitish stripes on them. Periodically, one of these would be popped into the ice-box and then brought out so that we could cut it open. The pink and beautiful inside was as crisp as any ice-cream that you could ever wish for.'

For Mother's birthday lunch the following day the party ate freshly caught *kefalia*, flathead mullet grilled over charcoal and, later, dinner of 'octopus and tiny cuttlefish that had been ensconced in the ice-box, followed by cold chicken and fruit'. The next day's disaster, when the *benzina* failed to start and supplies ran low, culminated in salvation by the redoubtable master of all work, Spiro. He appeared with the sunset in the bows of a fishing boat 'like a massive bulldog', with 'a whole roasted sheep on a spit and beside it a great basket containing all the fruits of the season'.

Vivid descriptions of a long gone Corfu evoke memories of other picnics carried by boat to hidden harbours on sunny pine-scented islands. On

Majorca and Menorca years ago we escaped the heaving tourist beaches to explore rocky coves only accessible from the sea, where we ate small fat tortillas bursting with fresh eggs and potatoes, still warm and melting in their cooking tins and, after, climbed the rocks to drowse under Aleppo pine trees, lulled by the soporific buzz of bees. In the Seychelles, we sailed a broad-beamed schooner round uninhabited islands and landed on strips of beach shielded by windswept palms, to cook long silvery king fish and hefty tuna on improvised spits over fires of drift wood and dried palm fronds. We ate them with garlic mayonnaise, whisked up quickly in an old jug by a ship's cook well used to improvisation.

Hong Kong summer weekends in the late 1970s and early 80s were spent on boats anchored around the islands in flat calm water by the High Island dam or close to the Chinese border in Deep Bay, where overnight stays meant the luxury of early morning waterskiing as the mist rose from basalt dark glassy water. Weekending boats ranged from the large junks owned by Hong Kong 'hongs', the great trading houses of the East, to privately owned gin palaces that, unlike the smaller vessels of lesser mortals, came with attached uniformed staff. Food was a competitive field even in days when, in spite of the wealth of Chinese food, all expatriate cooking suffered constraints on choice in imported foods. A butter lettuce from Stanley Market was the height of imported luxury. As small enterprising dealers began importing New Zealand meat or Italian olive oil and pasta for expat consumption the race for the most exotic ingredients was on and menu competition became a nightmare feature in the life of the shopper or caterer, both at home and at sea.

Pre-marriage days meant picnics on company junks where quantities of alcohol were quite irrelevantly supplemented by delicacies from the Mandarin Hotel Cake Shop, one of the few purveyors of imported food. Selections of Swiss-German cold meats and quiches, invariably followed by a deep apple pie with cinnamon and sultanas, reflected the origins and training of much of the Mandarin staff and were bought at premium prices to accompany the Mandarin's fresh French bread.

Once married and possessed of a small motor cruiser called *Go Liquid* (a financial rather than alcohol inspired allusion) and never having cooked much more than a boiled egg, this expat wife was on a steep learning curve. It was all too easy to be spoilt by the presence of A Chan, small but incredibly strong, her round face split by an enormous toothy smile, she had, for 20 years, cooked perfectly most of the food required by a long-term expatriate bachelor with a brother whose food business provided chilled food parcels of smoked salmon, cod roe and even Dover soles.

A Chan's picnic preparations went so far as parboiling potatoes, which unfortunately turned perfectly black after a few hours exposure to the air, to providing a fillet of beef carefully anointed and oiled for Sunday roasting in the miniscule galley on the boat. For me, an initial triumph with properly home-made mayonnaise (something that A Chan, for some reason, found difficult) and, a magical event for a novice cook, an experimental cheese soufflé that puffed like a mushroom cloud, encouraged careful study of Elizabeth David's books, a transformative wedding present. The same soufflé in time became the ultimate boat picnic show off, made in the unreliable gas oven with extra egg whites as insurance, and followed by lobsters ostentatiously positioned on deck in a large ice-filled champagne bucket.

This though is dinner party food, transported to the deck of a boat for sheer one-upmanship. It is not proper picnic food, which, on more normal days, might include hot soup in winter, tomato, onion or a strong consommé; cold in summer, a thin but spicy gazpacho that became, like the winter consommé, an alcoholic elevenses with the addition of a generous dose of vodka. Outstanding among more predictable soup, sandwich and cold meat menus were curries, carried in large flower-patterned Thermoses from the Chinese Emporium, the outlet for goods from mainland China. A Chan's Anglo-Indian style chicken curry came with fried onions, chopped apple and sultanas, or we collected the best takeaways from the scruffy, Formica-tabled and perpetually busy Indonesian restaurant in Happy Valley. Our order seldom varied: chicken curry 'no skin, no bone', beef *rendang*, shrimp sambal, pickled cucumber and *nasi goreng*, the Indonesian spicy fried rice with a unique taste wholly dissimilar to its supermarket imitations.

The Complete Asian Cookbook, Charmaine Solomon

'3 eggs; salt and pepper; oil for frying; 250g raw prawns; 500g pork or lean beef steak; 2 medium onions; 2 cloves garlic, crushed; ½ teaspoon dried shrimp paste (trasi); 4 cups cold cooked rice; 6 spring onions, thinly sliced; 2 tablespoons light soy sauce; 2 tablespoons onion flakes (fry in hot oil very thinly, evenly sliced onions until they are brown with all moisture cooked out – they can then be kept in jars); 1 green cucumber, thinly sliced.

Beat eggs with salt and pepper to taste. Heat very little oil in a frying pan and make an omelette with half the beaten eggs. Turn on to a plate to cool (do not fold). Repeat with remaining beaten eggs. When cool, put one omelette on top of the other, roll up and cut into thin strips.

Shell and de-vein prawns, cut beef or pork into fine strips. Chop onions roughly and blend to a paste in blender with garlic and trasi.

Heat 3 tablespoons of oil in a large frying pan or wok and fry the blended ingredients until cooked. Add prawns and meat to pan and fry, stirring constantly, until they are cooked. Ad 2 tablespoons more oil and when hot stir in the rice and spring onions, tossing and mixing thoroughly until very hot. Sprinkle with soy sauce and mix evenly. Serve garnished with strips of omelette, fried onion flakes and cucumber.'

Fynes Morison, a contemporary of Shakespeare and Marlowe, whose *Itinerary* is an account of his journeys and experiences around Europe and the Mediterranean during the 1590s, suffered shipboard food very different to the Durrells' when they lived in that part of the world. He found his voyage between Crete and Constantinople in 1597 'tedious to us, in that howsoever landing we had sometimes good dyet, yet while we were at Sea, we had no good victuals in the ship'. As usual things were much improved by the fortuitous discovery of liberal quantities of alcohol.

'For the Greeke Marriners feede of Onions, Garlike, and dried fishes, (one kind whereof they call Palamides, and the Italians call Palamito*) and in stead of a banket, they will give you a head of Garlick rosted in the ashes, and pleasantly call it a pigeon. With this and Bisket they content themselves, and these we were forced to eate, to find those in having omitted to provide any fresh meates, because they would not suffer a fier to be made in so small a Barke, wherewithal we might

---

*. Bonito or mackerelw

dress them. But after we had eaten Bisket and dried fishes, we had an unknown comfort of helpe to disgest them. For in our privat cabin, we had the head of a tun of Muskendine lying under our heads when we slept, with bundles of Reedes, to beate off the force of the waves, we taking one of the long Reedes, found meanes to pierce the vessel, and get good Wine to our ill fare, and drunke so merrily, that before wee came to our journies end, our former Reede became too short, so as we were faine to piece it with another.'

In 1827 the 1st Duke of Buckingham and Chandos chose to improve the ill-health brought on by his excessive size, his nickname was 'Le Gros Marquis', and escape the debts of excessive spending. Commissioning a ship, the *Anna Eliza*, he set off on an extraordinary mid-life grand tour of the Mediterranean. The ship was 96 feet long with a 48 man crew, a kennel for his dog on deck and a steam kitchen presided over by the Duke's Majorcan chef, Fontara; which suggests that the Duke's temporary exchange of situation from Stowe Park to ocean wave was hardly that of prince to pauper. Plenty of space was kept for the storage of wine and one of his travelling party, the Vicomte de Chabot, a French exile from the revolution, travelled ahead to France to buy delicacies for the table, supplementing English provisions that included a turtle. The turtle was probably one of the green turtles imported live from the Caribbean and, during early explorations of the New World, kept alive on board ships to provide vital protein for the sailors.

As a child I remember turtle soup still featuring on menus in restaurants like L'Aperitif in London's Jermyn Street and turtles of one species or their eggs are still hunted for food in spite of their threatened status. The *Gourmet Cookbook* of 1950, the source of a number of recipes that are liable to appal contemporary sensibilities, offers, from a choice of several similar, including a really distressing terrapin stew, the turtle steak (right). It is an adaptation of a classic French beef steak recipe. Mrs Beeton's clear turtle soup using sun-dried turtle meat has been discarded in favour of her mock turtle made with a calf's head. On reflection, it might be as easy today to acquire the former as the latter.

Turtle Steaks Marchand de Vin (Gourmet Cookbook)

Rub 6 individual turtle steaks with a damp cloth dipped in a little vinegar. Dip each steak into seasoned flour, in beaten egg, and finally in sieved bread crumbs. Heat 1.4 cup butter and stir in 1 tablespoon finely chopped shallots. Cook the steaks in this to a delicate brown on both sides. Pour over the browned steaks 1 cup Bordeaux and season with salt, pepper, and a dash of nutmeg. Cover the pan and simmer gently for 15 to 20 minutes. Dress the steaks on a hot platter and keep hot.

Reduce the sauce in the pan over a hot flame to almost nothing. Stir in ¼ cup rich beef stock, ½ cup sherry, and 1 cup thinly sliced mushrooms, cooked in a little butter. Taste for seasoning. Pour a little of the sauce over each steak and serve the rest in a sauceboat. Garnish with water cress.

Clear Mock Turtle Soup (Potage de Tortue, Fausse, Clair.)

½ a calf's head, 5 quarts of clear Second Stock (or water), 2 onions, 2 carrots, 1 turnip, a strip of celery, bouquet-garni (parsley, basil, marjoram, thyme, bay-leaf). 12 peppercorns, 4 cloves, 2 blades of mace, 2 glasses of sherry, 1 tablespoon of lemon-juice, ½ a lb of lean beef, ½ a lb of lean veal, the whites and shells of 2 eggs, salt.

Soak the head 24 hours in salt and water, changing it frequently. Then bone the head (the brains and tongue may be used for some other purpose), tie the meant in a thin cloth and break the bones into small pieces; put them into a stewpan, cover with cold water, add a tablespoonful of salt, let it boil up, strain, and was the head in cold water. Return the meat and bones to the stewpan, put in the stock and a dessertspoonful of salt, boil up, and skim well. Now add the prepared vegetables, herbs, peppercorns, cloves and mace, and when boiling, remove the scum, put on the cover and cook slowly for about 3 hours according to the size of the head. Strain, put the meat aside, and when the stock is cold remove the fat, and clarify with the coarsely chopped beef and veal and whites of eggs. Return to the saucepan, with the sherry, the lemon-juice and a little of the meat of the head, cut into small pieces. Add necessary seasoning, boil up and serve.

(Mrs Beeton's *Household Management*)

On Christmas Day 1827, the Duke was on board the *Anna Eliza* in port at Messina in Sicily. He had been unwell but was still keen that the festival should be celebrated in proper style.

> 'My ship's company had a plentiful hot dinner served to them, and my warrant-officers had another on the quarter-deck. My servants had a third. An allowance of beer was given them, as well as wine. In the evening I got two fiddles and a harp on board; a quart of warm punch per man was served out to the whole ship's company; dancing began and continued all evening. The men enjoyed themselves beyond measure'.

(Roberts and Morgan-Grenville, *No Ordinary Tourist*)

George Cheyne took a dim view of punch in his *Essay of Health and Long Life* in 1745, but punches and similar spirituous mixtures in one form or another flow through records of food and drink since the earliest times and particularly those of sailors.

'Next to Drams, no Liquor deserves more to be stigmatised and banished the repasts of the tender, valetudinary, and studious, than Punch. 'Tis a composition of such Parts, as not one of them is salutary or kindly to such constitutions, except the pure element, in it. The principal ingredient is Ru, Arrack, Brandy, or Malt Spirits ... The other principal part of the composition is the juice of oranges and lemons. And if we consider, that a lemon or orange could never be transported half seas over to us, without rotting or spoiling, if gathered when wholly ripe, we should have no great opinion of their juices.'

Mrs Beeton's Hot Punch (1839)

- 1/2 pint of rum
- 1/2 pint of brandy
- 1/4 lb. of sugar
- 1 large lemon
- 1/2 teaspoonful of nutmeg
- 1 pint of boiling water.

Mode. Rub the sugar over the lemon until it has absorbed all the yellow part of the skin, then put the sugar into a punchbowl; add the lemon-juice (free from pips), and mix these two ingredients well together. Pour over them the boiling water, stir well together, add the rum, brandy, and nutmeg; mix thoroughly, and the punch will be ready to serve. It is very important in making good punch that all the ingredients are thoroughly incorporated; and, to insure success, the processes of mixing must be diligently attended to.

Sufficient. Allow a quart for 4 persons; but this information must be taken cum grano salis; for the capacities of persons for this kind of beverage are generally supposed to vary considerably.

The young artist Sidney Parkinson, accompanied Joseph Banks, the naturalist and explorer, on Captain Cook's 1768 voyage to the South Pacific. Parkinson, before himself succumbing to dysentery, left a remarkable illustrated journal that provides some curious insights into a medicinally experimental-sounding ship's diet in which various turtles were some of the least bizarre components. By this time the means of avoiding the sailors' curse of scurvy were fairly well understood although there is a view that Cook, with his less reported belief in the anti-scorbutic efficacy of malt over fresh citrus fruit, was not as responsible for its decline as his legend would have it. Others like the Scottish doctor, James Lind, tested a variety of remedies including 'cyder', 'elixir of vitriol'* and 'a course of seawater', before confirming that 'the most sudden and visible good effects were perceived from the use of the oranges and lemons; one of those who had taken them being at the end of six days fit for duty.'

> Take of Sulphuric Acid three troy ounces;
> Fluid Extract of Orange Peel, one fluid ounce;
> Red Rose Leaves, two drachms;
> Boiling Water, one fluid ounce;
> Alcohol, a sufficient quantity.

> Add the acid gradually to half a pint of alcohol, and pour the boiling water upon the rose leaves; When both liquids have become cool, unite them, add the fluid extract and sufficient alcohol to make up the measure of eighteen fluid ounces. Mix thoroughly and filter.

> Elixir of vitriol, thus prepared, has a pleasant aromatic odor and flavour, and the beautiful red color of the rose leaves, heightened by the presence of the acid. It is miscible with water without turbidity, and a specimen, after long keeping, has deposited but a trace of sediment.

Parkinson's descriptions include some foods that may have been a better antidote against scurvy than others; fresh meat must certainly have been an improvement over salted and the explorers were ready and willing to try whatever came their way.

---

*. Elixir of Vitriol otherwise known as Aromatic Sulphuric Acid sounds a pretty refreshment in this version from *The American Journal of Pharmacy* of 1871.

'Tobiah, Obereah's favourite, being at dinner with us, and not seeming to like our provision, which was pork-pie, remembering that we had a large cuttle-fish, we ordered it to be brought; Tubora Tumaida coming in the mean time, although he said his belly was full, immediately seized on it as if it had been a dainty morsel, and, with another man, ate much of it quite raw; and having the rest roasted, he ate the greatest part of it; the remainder he put into two cocoa nuts, and sent it home with great care; so that, to all appearance, they value this fish, as much as some Englishmen do turtle, or a haunch of venison. When this fish was dressed it ate like stewed oysters, but not so tender. I have been told that this fish makes excellent soup. These people also are fond of dog's-flesh, and reckon it delicious food, which we discovered by their bringing the leg of a dog roasted to sell. Mr. Banks ate a piece of it, and admired it much. He went out immediately and bought one, and gave it to some Indians to kill and dress it in their manner, which they did accordingly. After having held the dog's mouth down to the pit of his stomach till he was stifled, they made a parcel of stones hot upon the ground, laid him upon them, and singed off the hair, then scraped his skin with a cocoa shell, and rubbed it with coral; after which they took out the entrails, laid them all carefully on the stones, and after they were broiled ate them .... nor did some of our people scruple to partake with them of this indelicate repast. Having scraped and washed the dog's body clean, they prepared an oven of hot stones, covered them with bread-fruit leaves, and laid it upon them, with liver, heart and lungs, pouring a cocoa-nut full of blood upon them, covering them too with more leaves and hot stones, and inclosed the whole with earth patted down very close to keep in the heat. It was about four hours in the oven, and at night it was served up for supper: I ate a little of it; it had the taste of coarse beef, and a strong disagreeable smell; but Captain Cook, Mr. Banks, and

Dr. Solander, commended it highly, saying it was the sweetest meat they had ever tasted; but the rest of our people could not be prevailed on to ate any of it. We have invented a new dish, which is as much disliked by the natives, as any of theirs is by us. Here is a species of rats, of which there are great numbers in this island; we caught some of them, and had them fried; most of the gentlemen in the bell-tent ate of them, and commended them much; and some of the inferior officers ate them in a morning for breakfast.'

After which, strange fish and a multitude of oysters sound tame indeed.

'Of fish, we found many different sorts, and a variety of beautiful shell-fish; among them three sorts of oysters; some were found in lagoons; some adhering to the mangrove; and others along the shore: large cavalhe, or scomber; large mullets, some flat-fish, a great number of small scombri; and skate or ray-fish; one of which, that we caught, was curiously marked on the back with polygons finely coloured, and another of an orbicular figure, with a blue grey-coloured back, and white belly, which tasted like veal; some other parts like beef; and the entrails as agreeable as turtle. We caught also turtles of a bright green colour, some of which weighed near four hundred pounds.'

Turtles continue to appear in seafarers' accounts as a desirably meaty change or adjunct to a fishy diet at sea. The sociologist Bengt Danielsson is described by Thor Heyerdahl during the famous Kon-Tiki expedition when in pursuit of a 'thumping big sea turtle' that was being attacked by a school of dolphins.

'Bengt as steward saw in his mind's eye endless meat dishes and the most delicious turtle soup. But the faster they rowed, the faster the turtle slipped through the water just below the surface, and they were not more than a hundred yards from the raft when the turtle suddenly disappeared without trace.'

Fish on the other hand were ready for martyrdom.

'Scarcely a day passed without at any rate, flying fish coming on board of their own accord. It even happened that large bonitos, delicious eating, swam on board with the masses of water that came from astern, and lay kicking on the raft when the water had vanished down between the logs as in a sieve. To starve to death is impossible.'

To die of thirst too is quite avoidable it seems, although the desperate methods used to avoid dehydration when water supplies become stale and low sound unappealing: 'chewing thirst-quenching moisture out of raw fish'. One is not surprised to read that 'It does not taste good if one has anything better to drink'. The alternative was marginally less stomach churning, the addition of 20-40 per cent of sea water added to fresh which successfully quenched thirst while a chance wave at breakfast taught the crew that the 'sickening taste of sea water' was much reduced by mixing it into a porridge with oats.

From starvation rations to bizarre excess; in *The Gastronomical Me* M. F. K. Fisher describes the Captain's dinner on the Italian freighter on which she travelled from France to America in 1932. The flying fish were again a constant presence, the sound of them slapping on water an accompaniment to a vast dinner sounding more like some mediaeval feast with a table centre piece of stuffed pheasants still in their feathers. Finally, the chef's pièce de résistance, a huge pink and white sugar replica of Milan Cathedral, slightly dusty and mended and lit from the inside. It was of course, never intended for eating but for applause. A surreal work of art of which the chef remained as inordinately proud as on its first showing many years before.

In 1935 Fisher was once again aboard ship, a comfortable German one 'at the same time subtly coarse and vulgar', with too regular a supply of extravagant food; foie gras, wild boar, and whipped cream, 'like a gluttonous dream'; ever to be hungry enough to enjoy it. The other passengers sound the stuff of nightmares or the caricature bad character of a John Buchan novel, raising an unending supply of brimming liqueur glasses in successive toasts to the picture of Hitler in the room until their monocles fell out.

The final First Class dinner on the *Titanic* ran to ten courses, including a palate cleansing *Punch Romaine* at number six, prior to roast squab and cress, asparagus vinaigrette, pâté de foie gras and celery and finally, Waldorf pudding, peaches in chartreuse jelly, chocolate and vanilla éclairs and French ice cream. In Third Class they thought themselves well off with pea soup, cabin biscuits, bread, fish in egg sauce or hotpot with potatoes, stewed apple and custard. In earlier days, third class passengers had been required to supply their own provisions for a sea journey.

Today's cruises, one hears, live up to the 'gluttonous dream' although old-fashioned menus offering solid dishes like Lobster Américaine Flambé or Châteaubriand also provide, as a sort of memento mori , a 'nutrition key' with details of calorie, fat and fibre contents.

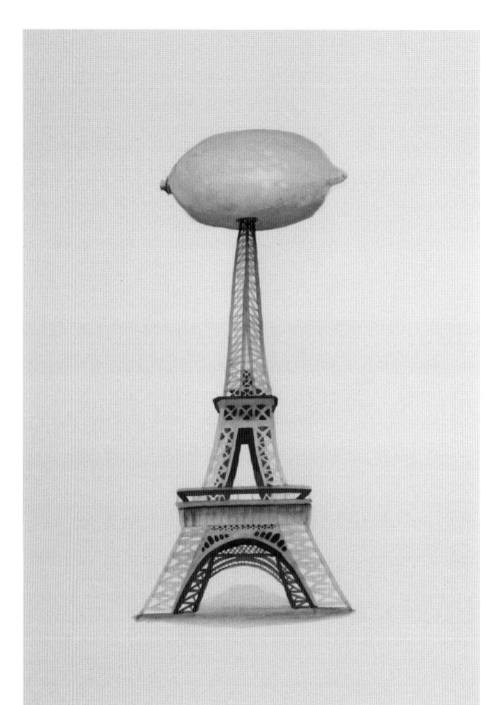

Picnics and Romance

Our wedding day was, unbeknownst to the bride, timed exactly for the honeymoon to fit neatly with that year's Monte Carlo Grand Prix. Luckily, I like motor racing and the weather was the best of early summer in the South of France. As I remember we drove one day up into the hills of Provence on an unplanned and circuitous route stopping at lunch time in a half-closed village for picnic supplies to supplement one of those large ceramic Fortnum and Mason pots, its cheerful sturgeon motif indicative of interior luxuries. A last minute wedding present from our best man, it still sits, topless now, in my kitchen, regularly refilled with grey Breton sea salt bought on other French journeys. We found a crackling fresh baton of bread, butter, lemons and a litre of wine easily enough. Perhaps we should have had vodka in those days before we learnt to fear drink driving and drunk drivers, but the wine fitted the sun and scene and dinner that night was already booked at the Hôtel du Cap d'Antibes. As I remember we had no knife and none was to be found in the few unshuttered shops, mostly as determinedly *fermé* as only afternoon in a French provincial village can achieve. Instead we managed with a metal nail file, the sort that used to be in the manicure sets that came in zipped leather cases, with other unnameable mysterious miniature blacksmiths' tools fascinating to children. Caviar was rarely so inelegantly consumed as we sat by the road breathing the scented Provençal air and revelled in a delicious excess of popping salty fishiness; building a wine-inspired future of castles in the air as we scraped the last eggs from the bottom of the pot.

Picnics lend themselves to romance or maybe it is the other way round but a romantic, and more so a sensual, seductive picnic, usually requires more careful planning to be a success than that provided ad hoc by caviar and sunshine. In *An Alphabet for Gourmets*, M. F. K. Fisher described what should have been the most perfect seductive dinner given for her by an expert in the field, a man married for the fifth time. The setting was immaculate, a candlelit patio, a beautifully laid table and a starry sky. Unfortunately the host had failed to take the weather into account, serving a hot, heavy meal on one of the hottest nights of the year. He had also failed to take into account that his guest was pregnant and had been his wife for several months. She describes the evening as 'thoroughly horrible'.

The midnight feast carefully contrived by Porphyro, with the help of the old nurse, Angela, in Keats's *St Agnes Eve*, is one of the most romantic of all picnics.

> Then by the bed-side, where the faded moon
> Made a dim, silver twilight, soft he set
> A table, and half anguish'd, threw thereon
> A cloth of woven crimson, gold and jet:-
> O for some drowsy Morphean amulet!
> The boisterous, midnight, festive clarion,
> The kettle-drum, and far-heard clarionet,
> Affray his ears, though but in dying tone:-
> The hall door shuts again, and all the noise is gone.
>
> While he from forth the closet brought a heap
> Of candied apple, quince, and plum, and gourd;
> With jellies soother than the creamy curd,
> And lucent syrops, tinct with cinnamon;
> Manna and dates, in argosy transferr'd
> From Fez; and spiced dainties, every one
> From silken Samarcand to cedar's Lebanon
> On golden dishes and in baskets bright
> Of wreathed silver; sumptuous they stand
> In the retired quiet of the night,
> Filling the chilly room with perfume light.

Whilst those well-travelled 'lucent syrops' and 'soother' jellies might owe their existence to poetic fancy, they gleam on in the mind's eye, and, with the jewel-like crystallised fruits, arranged for their beauty in the moonlight, encourage further flights of fantasy. The dates, fat and bursting, elegantly stuffed with nuts or almond paste; the metaphorical manna, who knows? A metaphor for bread? A sweet saffron coloured brioche perhaps? And more; gilded diamonds of marchpane, flavoured with rose water; orange lokum; sherbet to drink, or a smooth milk punch spiked with spirit; silver baskets of roasted pistachios; and tiny savoury pastries, barely a mouthful, flavoured with mint and coriander.

Of course none of it got eaten, unless by palsied old Angela or the mice, as Porphyro and his lover, Madeline, stole silently away from the castle into the freezing January night, while her father, Porphyro's sworn enemy, feasted in the hall with his blood-thirsty kinsmen.

And they are gone: ay, ages long ago
These lovers fled away into the storm.
That night the Baron dreamt of many a woe,
And all his warrior-guests, with shade and form
Of witch, and demon, and large coffin-worm,
Were long be-nightmar'd. Angela the old
Died palsy-twitch'd, with meagre face deform;
The Beadsman after thousand aves told,
For aye unsought for slept among his ashes cold.

Milk Punch (The Practical Housewife, Anon, 1860)

Peel the yellow zest from 3 lemons and place in a large bowl. Squeeze the lemons and pour the juice through a sieve onto the zest. Stir in 200 grams of granulated sugar, 500ml of water and 375ml of rum. Heat 123ml of whole milk to boiling point, pour over other ingredients, cover bowl and leave in a cool place for 24 hours. Line a sieve with two or three layers of butter muslin, place over a jug, and filter punch through the muslin, then pour into a clean bottle. Cork and keep in a cool place until required. Serve cold, in glasses or by ladling from a punch bowl.

Sir Kenelm Digby is best known for his 17th century cookbook *The Closet of the Eminently Learned Sir Kenelme Digbie Opened.* He was an eccentric intellectual of wide interests and something of a romantic figure, whether beloved, according to his own account, of Marie de Medici, or just much loved by the women he served who included Queen Henrietta Maria. His recipes are full of the exotic romance of Keats's imagined picnic and these strengthening tablets of properly aphrodisiac ingredients, pearls, musk and ambergris, unfortunately beyond the scope of most modern cooks.

Pleasant Cordial Tablets,
which are very comforting, and strengthen nature much

Take four ounces of blanched Almonds; of Pine kernels, and of Pistachios, ana, four Ounces. Erin-go-roots, Candid-Limon peels, ana, three Ounces, Candid Orange peels two Ounces, Candid Citron-peels four Ounces, of powder of white Amber, as much as will lie upon a shilling; and as much of the powder of pearl, 20 grains of Ambergreece, three grains of Musk, a book of leaf gold, Cloves and Mace, of each as much as will lie upon a three pence; cut all these as small as possible you can. Then take a pound of Sugar, and half a pint of water, boil it to a candy-height, then put in the Ambergreece and Musk, with three or four spoonfulls of Orange flower water. Then put in all the other things and stir them well together, and cast them upon plates, and set them to dry: when both sides are dry, take Orange-flower-water and Sugar, and Ice them.

My Lord of Denbigh's Almond March-Pane

Blanch Nut-Kernels from the Husks in the best manner you can. Then put them with a due proportion of Sugar, and a little Orange-flower, or Rose-water. When it is in a fitting uniform paste, make it into round Cakes, about the bigness of your hand, or a little larger, and about a finger thick; and lay every one upon a fine paper cut fit to it; which lay upon a table. You must have a pan like a tourtiere, made to contain coals on the top, that is flat, with edges round about to hold in the coals, which set over the Cakes, with fire upon it. Let this remain upon the Cakes, till you conceive, it hath dryed them sufficiently for once; which may be within a quarter of an hour; but you take it off two or three times in that time, to see you scorch not the outside, but only dry it a little. Then remove it to others, that lye by them; and pull the Papers from the first, and turn them upon new Papers. When the others are dryed enough, remove the pan back to the first, to dry their other side: which being enough, remove it back to the second, that by this time are turned, and laid upon new Papers. Repeat this turning the Cakes, and changing the Pan, till they are sufficiently dry: which you must not do all at once, least you scorch them: and though the outside be dry, the inside must be very moist and tender. Then you must Ice them thus: Make a thick pap with Orange flower or Rose-water, and purest white Sugar: a little of the whites of Eggs, not above half a spoonful of that Oyl of Eggs, to a Porrenger full of thick Pap, beaten exceeding well with it, and a little juyce of Limons. Lay this smooth upon the Cakes with a Knife, and smoothen it with a feather. Then set the pan over them to dry them. Which being if there be any unevenness, or cracks or discolouring, lay on a little more of that Mortar, and dry it as before. Repeat this, till it be as clear, and smooth, and white, as you would have it. Then turn the other sides, and do the like to them. You must take care, not to scorch them: for then they would look yellow or red, and they must be pure, white and smooth like Silver between polished and matte, or like a looking Glass. This Coat preserves the substance of the Cakes within, the longer moist. You may beat dissolved Amber, or Essence of Cinnamon, with them.

Food for Lovers, a *1977* book with recipes by Katie Stewart and Ken Lo, is disappointingly short on fantastic dishes although the introduction discusses the demerits of various purported aphrodisiacs, many of which, like Spanish Fly or cantharides can be lethal.[*] The book suggests that a cucumber salad should be avoided at your romantic picnic; according to the Elizabethan physician and traveller Andrew Boorde, it 'restrayneth veneryousnes, or lassyuyousnes, or luxuryousnes'. He may have known what he was talking about since he was eventually convicted of keeping loose women in his lodgings at Winchester, and, in other stipulations on the importance of cleanliness in the house and especially the kitchen, was

---

[*]. Spanish Fly was finally banned from sale in the spice markets of Morocco only in the 1990s and is still advertised for sale on the internet. Its deadly effects were demonstrated when the Marquis de Sade poisoned two prostitutes with copiously laced aniseed sweets, three others, who perhaps did not like aniseed, survived. As recently as 1954, in London, Arthur Ford gave doctored coconut bonbons to an office colleague with whom he was infatuated and managed to poison both her and a friend who ate them too. Those looking for a moral might suggest that eating really disgusting sweets is bad for the health as the drug appears not to have a taste that needs powerful disguise. Alan Davidson provides a more amusing anecdote from Moroccan research on the use of the aphrodisiac. He 'dissolved into laughter and, between laughs, related how his wife had once added some to a pan of spaghetti which she was boiling. When she came to serve this, she found that every single strand of spaghetti was standing bolt upright in the pan.' (Alan Davidson, *Oxford Companion*)

well ahead of his time. The authors of *Food for Lovers* believe that picnics have always been a favourite pursuit of the amorous but their lovers' picnics, divided into those suitable for rich, poor, hurried, or not, sound a great deal more depressing than their indoor meals. It is hard to imagine that 'Pickled or Soused Herrings with Rice Salad', beer or cider and fresh plums would encourage the poverty stricken to amatory adventures; or that salami or pizza for the hurried lover, in 'your basket with a pretty cloth', would produce summits of passion; although 'luscious peaches' sound quite nice. The lover with time to spare can manufacture 'chicken balls' and a 'pineapple dessert' for a picnic which sounds to me like the bitter end.

Edward Lear captures a far more romantic picnic, a honeymoon too.

The Owl and the Pussycat

The Owl and the Pussycat went to sea
In a beautiful pea-green boat,
They took some honey, and plenty of money,
Wrapped up in a five pound note.
The Owl looked up to the stars above,
And sang to a small guitar,
"O lovely Pussy! O Pussy, my love,
What a beautiful Pussy you are, you are, you are,
What a beautiful Pussy you are."
Pussy said to the Owl "You elegant fowl,
How charmingly sweet you sing.
O let us be married, too long we have tarried;
But what shall we do for a ring?"
They sailed away for a year and a day,
To the land where the Bong-tree grows,
And there in a wood a Piggy-wig stood
With a ring at the end of his nose, his nose, his nose,
With a ring at the end of his nose.
"Dear Pig, are you willing to sell for one shilling your ring?"
Said the Piggy, "I will"
So they took it away, and were married next day

By the Turkey who lives on the hill.
They dined on mince, and slices of quince,
Which they ate with a runcible spoon.
And hand in hand, on the edge of the sand
They danced by the light of the moon, the moon, the moon,
They danced by the light of the moon.

While the mince sounds worthy but hardly exciting, there are recipes for quince and meat stews or quince with meat stuffing in Iranian cuisine and the quince itself has long been considered a fruit of love. The ancient Greeks held the quince sacred to Aphrodite, the goddess of love to whom Paris gave the golden apple of the Hesperides. Golden apples were synonymous with quinces, appearing also in Norse mythology as the food of immortality of the gods and, most probably, as the 'apples' of the *Song Of Solomon*. There are innumerable recipes for quince jellies, preserves and tarts in Middle Eastern and older English cookbooks and the honeymooners knew what they were doing with their supply of honey. Soyer tells us the quince possesses 'the most beneficial qualities' and 'marvellous virtues.'

'This fruit, so much extolled, was preserved by placing it with its branches and leaves in a vessel, afterwards filled with honey or sweet wine'. (Alexis Soyer, *Food, Cookery and Dining in Ancient Times*)

> 'In the best stories, the standard bill of fare is, I believe, cold venison pie, a good red wine, a couple of apples and some nuts...'
> 'Venison pie? It is one of the great alfresco delicacies. I have, ever since I put away childish things, made a firm rule: I will eat well prepared indoor things outdoors, and suitably delicious outdoor food, indoors; I will not, however, put myself in the double jeopardy of eating outdoor food outdoors. If I'm to suffer ants, spiders, dirt on my hands, and stones under my backside, I must have a touch of civilisation to take the curse off it. I'm not so degenerate as to insist on the wicker basket

and the red-and-white-checkered cloth – just degenerate enough to be convinced that everything tastes better if you have them.

At any rate venison is the archetypal pie that everything else is as easy as. You take a pie plate large enough to accommodate the remainder of your venison stew (which you have made with a good red-wine marinade plus some onions and mushrooms – but without potatoes, dumplings, carrots, parsnips or rutabagas). Next you line the plate with plain pastry, put in the stew, add a top crust, crimp the edge, cut a round hole in the centre, and bake till the pastry is nicely browned. You then cool it in the tin, wrap it in foil, and throw it in your knapsack. With a Cabernet, if you can afford it – or a four liter jug of red plonk, if you can carry it – there is no sickness that destroyeth in the noonday against which you will not have at least a fighting chance. *In vino veritas. Prosit!'*

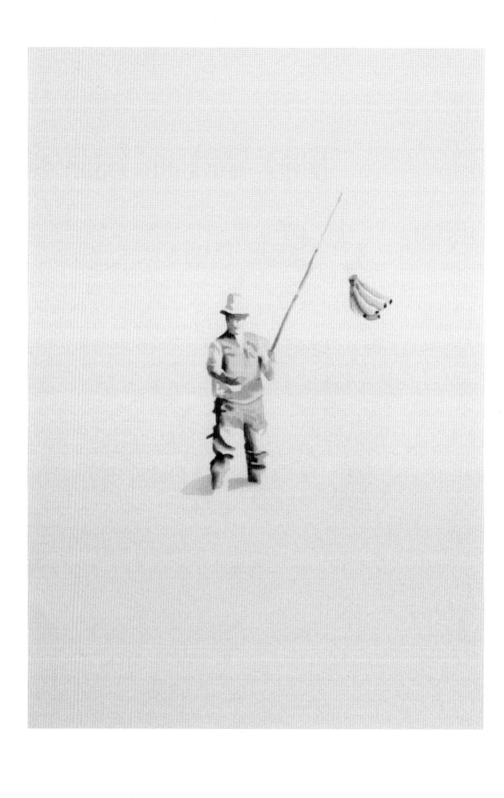

Home, Work and Tradition

We have a vision of rural life in villages and country towns between the late 18th and early 20th centuries; more or less romantically melancholic; more or less accurate; more or less summonsed by the romantic poets, Hardy's Wessex novels, Eliot's country villages and the encouraging illustrations beguiling young searchers of volumes in old nursery bookshelves or provincial second hand bookstores. True histories of country life and livelihood that include the everyday, drudgery spiked with high days and holidays, brief moments of relaxation in the endless cycle of agricultural work, are harder to find.

21st century village traditions are often perpetuated courtesy more of the imaginations of energetic rural migrants than the down to earth memories of older inhabitants. Many of the outdoor leisure activities we picture as part of the bygone life of rural inhabitants have little to do with a reality of hardship and poverty where work and play were less clearly delineated than in the waged occupations of the cities. Agricultural labourers for instance seldom had time for village cricket and 19th century football appears to have been predominantly an urban sport. 'Well, the only cricket played in the village was by the local squire or farmer or big nob that could get some of the school masters or higher nobs round the village in his team.' (Barry Reay, *Rural Englands*)

The 20th and 21st century stalwarts of the flower shows, the church fêtes, the village cricket and the garden openings are supporting activities that may not have been those of the earlier owners of their thatched cottages. Their leisure activities were the decorative stitching imposed on the pattern of work or the enforced idleness of unemployment. Nevertheless the village church tastefully decorated for a flower or harvest festival revives memories of long-gone lifestyles vested in the soil and punctuated by seasonal and religious festivals in which the whole community participated. Prayers and ceremonies to propitiate Mother Nature are as timeless and universal as the celebrations of her generosity and the grumbling wakes for her failures and foibles so enjoyed by any gathering of farmers.

An outdoor life has always involved eating in the open. The ploughman or carter out in the chill air with his bit of year round bread and cheese, eked out if he was lucky with a fresh onion from his garden in season, or a pint of ale from the farmer on wage days, is seldom the stuff of poetry. It is the warm glow of summer, hayfields, harvest and gleaning days, that is lyrically portrayed by poets and painters; the days when 'Every blade of grass, each leaf, each separate floret and petal, is an inscription speaking of hope.' (Richard Jefferies, *The Life of the Fields*). As urban populations grew in the 19th century, whole families came from Midland towns for working holidays 'hopping' in Kent while local agricultural families across the country took to the fields with the farmer and his wife. Her arrival in a well-provisioned gig added to the atmosphere of communal plenty that eschewed thoughts of the winter to come and made a festivity of food and drink shared in the shade by summer fields.

Pasties of one sort and another have been popular lunches for farmers and labourers all over the country for hundreds of years. These days there are chains of stalls and bakeries selling ranges of 'original' pasties. The best known are Cornish pasties whose heavy crimped pastry edges are said to have been made so to keep tin miners dirty hands away from the pasty's meat and vegetable stuffing. The contaminated crust was then discarded.

Cornish Pasty 1922, St Ives

Flour ½ lb; lard or dripping 3oz; a pinch of salt; water to make a fine dough about 1gill (2½ liquid ounces). Uncooked beef steak ½lb; uncooked calf's liver ¼lb; uncooked potatoes 2; onion 1 large one; turnip 1 medium sized one; carrot 1 large or 2 small ones. Pepper and salt.

To bake 1 hour; at first in a good oven to raise the pastry and then in a very moderate oven to cook the meat and vegetables.

Roll out the dough fairly thin, cut in squares.

Chop the steak and liver finely, mix together and season.

Peel or scrape and slice the potato, onion, turnip and carrot. Mix and season the vegetables.

Put a layer of vegetables on half of each square of pastry and some of the chopped meat on top.

Brush the edges of the pastry with white of egg, fold the plain half over the meat and pinch the edge well together.

Bake as above.

N.B. – It is important to close the edges neatly and closely, so that no steam escapes, and to use uncooked meat and vegetables. The contents cook in their own juices, so after the first few minutes require a very moderate oven. The above amounts make 2 large or 3 medium- sized pasties.

(Good Things in England)

Atwood Clark's *Country Mix – Reminiscences of Rural Life and Sport in 19th Century England* draws on memories of South West England, in particular the Wiltshire villages, the downs and the rivers, close to where I live. The impenetrable Wiltshire accent he transcribes to give such character to some of his stories and best read aloud for understanding, only lives on now in the vocal shades and inflections of the most elderly speakers.

'Elevenses'. Blessed word! The workers have been thinking of it for an hour or more, and it was the exception rather than the rule for them to swallow a draught of anything liquid until the sun was high. If you did you would be thirsty all day... there is a rattle of wheels from the farm gig, driven by the farmer's wife, with a brace of 'bustious' boys of walking age perched beside her. With them are the half of a forty-pound cheese, a large 'batch' of bread, and an eighteen-gallon cask of home-brewed beer.

As each mower 'cuts out' he sets the blade of his scythe forward for safety into the uncut grass... Then wiping his forehead, and his mind concentrating on one great central thought, he makes for the gateway. Arrived, he notes a dissolving cluster of women who are bearing full jars and baskets from the gig. There is the moisture he craves and a cask with a tap already inserted. Beer! His wife meets him and hands an uncorked jar. He nods briefly, draws his hand across sticky, clammy lips, and lifts the familiar vessel... The old gods must have had attractive temporal joys to offer mortals if they had better things to give than the all-absorbing ecstasy of that draught.

There is a laugh from some young ones when one of the older men, who in passing the gig halted for a moment to view the cheese, which is being cut into mighty chunks by the farm mistress, and then lowered his head and peered. 'Fine cheese thickee, missis. Zee wur mousies's bin.' The laugh from the others is followed by affirmative murmurs, for every countryman knows that if there is a great pile of cheeses in the storage loft and a rare mouse finds its way to them and finally, after inspection, nibbles one, the cheese selected for the honour is surely the finest of them all. The common mouse is truly the best judge of good cheese in the world.

Summer work and rewards must have seemed another country as winter took it's freezing hold, although the following story from the lambing season of around 1810 obviously gave much amusement to its aged teller, in retrospect.

As things turned out they were weather-bound for four days before being able to cross three snowdrifted miles to the homestead.

'Thur wur nout ter do so us taarked and sumtime sung ims. But Zeb ee ad a vice wuss nor anny owd craw. Twur drefful ter ear un, an'our bellies wor emptier nor anny drum. Zeb ee ad korns an gat cauld veet as well, so ee taaked orf 'is bootses an' wropt is veet en a bit of ould zack. Wied bin boorwin'into thick straw (an troid ter ate un, us wor that thrawed) vor vour nights. On the laarst Zeb ee groned an snoared turble. Oi cudn't slape a winksie; oi wur that craavin' vor vittals.

Moi 'and cum gainst wun ov Zeb's bootses an oi thort twud be bettern nor nout, so oi toikes moi knoife an cuts orf most ov topsoide on im. Oi sloices thickee inter teeny bitses an chews thickee arl noight vore oi gits un daown. Thort ter ate the soal on un vore morning, but shipherd ee rousts up an' as a moind ter taaka looksee outside. Then er vound thick bit ov boot as oi'd lef un. Proper stark chap wor Zeb, an' vore oi cud move ee ad oi vast. Eer eld oi toight an' ad orf wum ov moi bootses. The ee cut orf top loike oi ad dun ter issen an chewd us as ef a loiked un. All toime ee luked main sour at oi an' simmed 'mazed wi honger soides. Oi wuz yung an tender those days an oi gits praaper veared, twuz oi. So oi thort twuz toime ter say as us ad better kill owd Blossom vor ter ate. Laks! Then oi thort ee was gwine ter murder oi roight smart; but ee onny made a drefful vaice an laned across oi an' gritted 'is toothen and maaked a nise loike a girt dog an' cussed oi. The er sed: "Oi'll zee tis theesen wot es ate vore oid vace maister wi bits o' Blossom insoide oi." Ee luked loike Bellsbub, oi tell ee.'

(Atwood Clark, *Country Mix*)

As to the river of the *Reminiscences*, it is the Kennet, also part of my fishing memories, although as much for summer picnic teas as great catches. Comfortably warm afternoons with older, more expert, fishing friends, free with teaching advice as to flies, casts, strategy; with quicker eyes for a trout, seen too late by me as he flicks his tail, speeding towards invisibility. Teas were simple enough, freshly made flaky little sausage rolls, cakes by Mr Kipling, whichever iced slice the current favourite of our host and delicious bottled lemonade, one of those with pretensions to home-made style. The point was as much the break as the food, an excuse for lying idle, horizontal, dozy, under the summer sky in the warm hay-smelling grass, before dragging ourselves up again to the business in hand; as often catching the bank; once as an unfortunate bet, an unsuspecting water rat; or a 'filthy' grayling; or as our target, the shy shining brown trout.

Views on the grayling do differ; Alfred E. T. Watson points out that 'Grayling are not bad eating, if properly cooked – that is, split open and grilled'. Izaak Walton was impressed more by their medicinal properties:

> 'The fat of an Umber or Grayling, being set, with a little honey,
> a day or two in the sun, in a little glass, is very excellent against
> redness or swarthiness, or anything that breeds in the eyes.'
> (Izaak Walton, *The Compleat Angler*)

Truth be told few fish straight from the river taste too bad with skin charred instantly on a throwaway barbecue, if such things are allowed, and a dash of salt and lemon. With the introduction into rivers of fat bred rainbow and brown trout, the delicate and delicious wild brown is ever rarer. Far and few in the Kennet are the wild four and five pounders of the late 19th century when Atwood Clark wrote of 'Kennet Monsters' that 'cut as pink as any sea-trout... and tasted better'.

'Anglers Roast Trout

Scour, wash, open and clean the fish as usual; then cut off their heads, score them lightly, and pepper and salt them inside and out; cut one or more branches (sweet birch is best), and stick the fish upon the twigs, running the twig along the upper side of the back-bone, hold the branch before the fire; by watching the inside of the fish it is easy to see when they are done.'

(The Unrivalled Cook and Housekeepers Guide, Mrs Washington)

> 'What say you, scholar, to the providence of an old angler? Does not this meat taste well? And was not this place well chosen to eat it? For this sycamore-tree will shade us from the sun's heat.' (*The Compleat Angler*)

Eiffel Tower Lemonade made from concentrated crystals is the picnic beverage, precursor to today's boutique mixes, that has stuck most in the memories of children of the late 19th and early 20th century, in company with sandwiches and little iced cakes sprinkled with hundreds and thousands.

> 'When I was a child, almost 60 years ago, Swindon had its Trip week. All who worked 'inside' were transported to seaside destinations by special Trip trains. The longest journeys to Penzance and St Ives left late in the evening and arrived before breakfast. The highlight of the journey was food, sandwiches, tea in a Thermos for the grown ups and lemonade made with Eiffel Tower crystals for the children (no buffet cars on Trip trains) – and delight of delight, Butter Puffs and triangular cream cheeses.' (*Wiltshire, Within Living Memory*)

Eiffel Tower advertisements were evocative and persuasive:

> 'Partly prepared in sunny Sicily from ripe, fragrant, luscious Messina Lemons, the choicest Lemons the world produces.
> Scores of peasants gather the Lemons from the trees, they are then taken direct from the Lemon Orchards into the Factory to commence their transformation into 'Eiffel Tower' Concentrated Lemonade. In this way thousands and thousands of bushels of the Finest Lemons are used every year. It is by this careful selection of the finest fruit only that the delicious flavor of 'Eiffel Tower' Lemonade is obtained.
> This delicious beverage is pre-eminently the best drink for children, because of its health-giving properties.'

And:

'As supplied to the House of Commons'

As it turned out, however delicious and however many MPs Eiffel Tower refreshed, it barely contained lemon at all, let alone the 38,000,000 per year claimed by the the makers of the 'Concoction', against whom a judgment was upheld in 1901. On analysis it had been found instead to contain 'about 40 per cent. of tartaric acid, 44 per cent. of cane sugar, 5 per cent. of oil of lemon and coloring matter, and 2 per cent. of water.' Justice O'Brien, for the court, decreed that 'There can be no possible escape from the conclusion that the article was held out to the public as made from lemon juice and that the beverage formed by its admixture with water was lemonade. As neither representation was true and the product was but an imitation or simulation of lemonade, the verdict is amply sustained.'   (*New York Times*, 2nd May 1901)

The concentrated drink that added to the problems of the *Three Men in a Boat* sounds very much like Eiffel Tower:

'I reminded him that there was concentrated lemonade in the hamper, and a gallon-jar of water in the nose of the boat, and that the two only wanted mixing to make a cool and refreshing beverage.

Then he flew off about lemonade, and "such-like Sunday-school slops", as he termed them, ginger-beer, raspberry syrup, &c., &c. He said they all produced dyspepsia, and ruined body and soul alike, and were the cause of half the crime in England.'

The Idris soft drinks factory was another source of ready-made lemonade and a ginger beer that still bears the Idris name although now manufactured by Britvic. The Idris factory was the site of a landmark strike in 1911 by the women workers in support of their demands for better conditions. They worked 'ankle deep in poorly drained water', and drank tea in their break that was 'boiled from the same water that had already been used to slop down the floor'. They walked out of the factory singing:

'Oh you great King in the palace,
And you statesman at the top;
When you're drinking soda water,
Or imbibing ginger pop;
Think of some who work at Idris,
For very little pay;
And who only get nine bob for a most unpleasant job.
A lack a day! A lack a day!'

(Juliet Nicholson)

Real home-made lemonade is delicious and not complicated to make but for some reason always seems an effort for something that disappears so quickly. Mrs Beeton and Constance Spry supply similar simple recipes; this is a combined version:

Real home-made lemonade

- The juice of 4 lemons
- The thinly pared zest of 2 lemons
- 3 tablespoons of sugar
- 1 quart boiling water
- Sprigs of mint
- Ice
- Fresh slices of lemon

Put juice, zest and sugar in a jug and pour in boiling water. Leave to stand until cooling, then strain. Cool completely and add mint and lemon slices at least an hour before serving.

Ginger beer in its non-alcoholic form is straightforward, requiring only some waiting time. The proper old-fashioned and potentially strongly alcoholic ginger beer that was so popular in the 19th century is a different matter; it is made using a ginger beer plant, a peculiar and rather revolting yeasty composite that can still be bought quite easily via the internet.

This is the recipe from *The Gentle Art of Cookery* using fresh yeast and sugar for fizz.

Ginger Beer

One ounce of bruised ginger, two pounds of
white sugar, two ounces of cream of tartar,
one lemon sliced.

Put all these into a large earthenware pan and
pour over them two gallons of boiling water.
When nearly cold, put one teaspoonful of
yeast spread on toast. Bottle in twenty-four
hours, and tie down the corks.

Memoirs of English country childhoods highlight yearly Sunday or village school outings, picnics and rare day trips to the nearest seaside.

'We walked a lot in our youth and thought nothing of two and a half miles to reach the top of the Cherhill Downs, carrying food, drink and a tray on which we would slide down the green slopes, then climb back to the top, ready to slide down again. In the evening, once a week, we were sent to Beehive, it was the junior branch of the Abstainers. All of us children signed The Pledge, vowing never to touch strong drink, then we were shown slides on a magic lantern. One thing I could never fathom out was the Abstainers' outing. Practically the entire town set off in a special train about six o'clock in the morning for a day at the seaside, returning home about 10pm by which time all the men were very merry and they had lots of empty bottles in their coat pockets. The Abstainers' outing was very popular.'

(Wiltshire, Within Living Memory)

In Cider with Rosie, Laurie Lee remembers a similar sounding choir outing in the 1920s by charabanc to Weston-super-Mare.

> 'Mothers with pig buckets stuffed with picnics, children with cocoa-tin spades and fathers with bulging overcoats lined entirely with clinking bottles'. Once arrived, the village women hired chairs on the muddy sand and complained about Weston tea. 'It's made from the drains, I reckon', while the men sought out the pubs. 'Hey, Jake, Steve; let's go and have a wet.'

Lee describes Harvest Festival in the days when 'the Church followed the plough very close' in more than prayer book headings and both were at the centre of village life and lives.

> 'Then how heavily and abundantly was our small church loaded; the cream of the valley was used to decorate it. Everyone brought of his best from field and garden; and to enter the church on Harvest morning was like crawling head first into a horn of plenty, a bursting granary, a vegetable stall, a grotto of bright flowers. The normally bare walls sprouted leaves and fruits, the altar great stooks of wheat, and ornamental loaves as big as cartwheels stood parked by the communion rails. Bunches of grapes, from the Squire's own vines, hung blue from the lips of the pulpit. Gigantic and useless marrows abounded, leeks and onions festooned the pews, there were eggs and butter on the lectern shelves, the windows were heaped with apples, and the fat round pillars which divided the church were skirted with oats and barley.'

My family on both sides are Wiltshire born and bred; both families fledging long lines of local worthies and Members of Parliament of greater or lesser standing. A local Women's Institute memoir describes the Jubilee celebrations of 1935 and the Coronations of 1937 and 1953 in the village on my grandfather's estate. What a relief to read that 'Major and Mrs John Morrison were very generous with money and food, so that the workers' wives and families would have a really good day of fun and frivolity'.

My grandfather had a track record in fun and frivolity. At the celebration of his coming of age in December 1927, a luncheon was held on one of the farms 'in a spacious building that had been decorated effectively with flowers and evergreens'. By the time the company sat down to a meat tea in a marquee that afternoon, the numbers had swelled to 800 of the employees of the estate and their families. Music was played during tea, including, in December, *One Summer Night* (on a melody by Dvorak) and a 'Graceful Dance' called '*Winsome Winnie*'. An entertainment was given by three performers from London; a ventriloquist, a conjurer and a purveyor of story and song. Afterwards there was a choice, in three separate rooms, of dancing, a whist drive or community singing. Frolics indeed, and party bags. Astonishingly each guest was presented with a framed, autographed photograph of the birthday boy.

Grandpa's heir, my Uncle James, celebrated his 21st in 1951 in the aftermath and economy of war but still achieved 150 for lunch in a marquee followed by sports, tea and dancing later for 500 on the floodlit lawns. For 'Gents over 60' the sport was 'Drinking half a pint of beer through a straw'.

Grandpa, Uncle James and his eldest son also had coming of age celebrations on their Scottish estate. In 1979, the marquee for my cousin's 21st blew down in a gale the night before. Relocated to the village hall, the company ate venison, chicken and ham salad, fruit salad and cream and drank Royal Chevalier Blanc de Blancs. The oldest estate employee made a speech remembering the celebrations for both earlier generations. For the first, he had been given the day off school for the sports. 'I remember clearly coming from Craigens by horse and cart and receiving a great luxury in those days, a tin of chocolates in a Morrison tartan box'. At the second in 1957, 'We celebrated Mr James' coming of age in a marquee in the Square. We were lavishly entertained to lunch catered by Fraser McArthur from Port Ellen. It was not so long after the war and whisky was not the freely available commodity it is today. It was however generously provided for the coming-of-age and I remember acting for a time as ambulance man ferrying casualties from the catering tent to the stalls in the old stable which had been well strawed for the occasion.'

The estate sports continued as a yearly event during most of my childhood summers in Islay and included a meat tea for all participants of rather dreaded cold venison, more pleasingly followed by a great many excellent cakes and the usual bottled orange squash of the time which smelt and tasted like sugared tin.

My father was another Wiltshire Member of Parliament, for the Devizes constituency. I don't know if he ever ate one, but the Devizes Pie, a sort of brawn, might make an unusual addition to a picnic. Calf's head is no longer popular in this country and positively shunned since CJD or mad cow disease hit the headlines. Contemporary recipes transform all that interesting offal into 'any leftover cold meat'. Not at all the same thing. This recipe comes from the *Magazine of Domestic Economy* of 1836 republished in Florence White's 1931, *Good Things in England*.

Devizes Pie

Boil a calf's head, cut it into very thin slices, with some of the brains.

Add slices of pickled tongue, sweetbread, lamb, veal, a few slices of bacon, and some hard-boiled eggs.

Put them in layers in a piedish with plenty of seasoning between each of cayenne, white pepper, allspice and salt.

Fill up the dish with rich gravy that will jelly when cold.

Cover with a flour-and-water paste; make a hole in the middle.

Bake in a slow oven for about one hour.

And when perfectly cold, take off the crust, and turn the pie out upon a dish; and garnish with parsley and pickled eggs cut in slices.

On Trains and Aeroplanes

'Travellers in these times are reverting to the old-fashioned habit of taking their journey food with them, some actuated by motives of economy if the party be numerous, others by the discomforts of that dark and perilous pilgrimage from remote parts of a swaying train to the crowded restaurant car. Some have a preference for the food of their own choice, others would limit the opportunity of the hostile microbe.'

'The travellers' food basket, equipped in some such ways as are here suggested, will render its owners independent of time and place, fortified against hunger and thirst, immune to the extortions and insolence of officials, and they will be fresh and ready on arrival to enjoy the lovely sights and gay adventures awaiting them...'

(Agnes Jekyll, *Food for Travellers*)

We had a friend in well-padded expatriate Hong Kong days who was reputed, I never saw him at it, always to fly economy, well sustained by a first class picnic. Champagne, vodka or a decent wine were obtainable on board to lubricate carry on food consisting of a largish tin of Beluga caviar, a lemon and some plain biscuits, Bath Olivers or the like. With this he was entirely content although I believe the menu was occasionally varied with a one of those small Kilner jars of foie gras.

I have been on plenty of flights when a pot of caviar would have been a highly welcome addition to the economy menu and sadly far too few in first class when caviar used to be a menu standard. I have never, however, achieved much more of a picnic than a couple of apples although, before those tinned American mixes became de riguer, I used to carry a small scent bottle filled with all the spices necessary to improve a bland drinks trolley Bloody Mary or several.

According to Digby Anderson: 'There is one occasion when "self-catering" is essential: on long aeroplane flights. Obviously one can't eat the unpleasant things provided.'

For 'young fogeys' he suggests 'A full six-course dinner in a wicker hamper. First, a challenging hors d'oeuvre such as oysters: a dozen or two packed in damp seaweed and opened just before serving (don't forget the oyster knife, the stewardesses never have one). Later, perhaps a nourishing mutton daube with anchovies (piping hot from a Thermos). Why not end with walnuts? Since one object of the exercise is to shame the airline, noisy and smelly dishes are a good idea.'

As the author points out, 'All this is equally possible on long-distance trains or (he imagines) coaches.' As for picnics in general, 'they enable you to eat well in places which are otherwise out of your control'. He adds to this list: hospitals; Germany; and 'self-catering' apartments, especially in California.

M.F.K. Fisher's descriptions of eating on trains, boats and planes portray the potential pleasures and horrors of travelling food and the need to improve on the rations provided.

Newly widowed in 1941, en route to stay with friends in Mexico, she suffered breakfast and lunch, on a delayed flight, in almost immediate succession. The breakfast, 'those limp cellophane envelopes of hot egg and meat were the most disgusting things I had ever seen', is all too familiar, but she made the best of a bad job with her lunch. We have all deconstructed nasty sandwiches in the attempt to make something edible out of their various parts. She was intensely proud of the neat sandwich she made with the chicken and ham contents of two of their kind, while carefully avoiding the remaining cardboard packages on her tray. As Digby Anderson suggests any such successful inventiveness with today's in-flight meals and 'icy sandwiches' is unlikely. It is better to follow Miss

Fisher's example only in more liquid forms of refreshment. The most encouraging part of her lunch was clearly the large slug of bourbon from her flask, slightly diluted with airline water. Alcohol so often puts a rosier glow on things.

As it turned out the gastronomic efforts of this particular airline were not yet exhausted. Shortly before landing, and, fortified with another slug from her flask, Fisher was presented with a beribboned cellophane box full of fruit and enclosing a paper slip that said: 'You may eat this with carefree abandon, for it has been washed and scrubbed and rub-a-dub-dubbed.'

Anthony Trollope's 1869 description of the railway sandwich in *He Knew He Was Right* leads the reader to awareness that contemporary railway catering has returned to its roots: 'the real disgrace of England is the railway sandwich, that whited sepulchre, fair enough outside, but so meagre, poor, and spiritless within, such a thing of shreds and parings, with a dab of food'.

When we were young, things were different or seemed so. Our winter day trips by train to London from Wiltshire meant easing the old-fashioned stiffness of Rowes tweed coats with velvet collars and velvet hats with dining car silver service breakfasts where white coated waiters offered porridge or cereal, followed by bacon, mushrooms, eggs and toast and marmalade. Toasted tea cakes on the 4.30 from Paddington return were accompanied by those little pots, magical for children, of honey, apricot and strawberry jams, eaten at white clothed tables lighted by maroon shaded lamps. Those dining cars were the nationalised successors to the pre-ordered picnic baskets delivered to passengers in pre-war days and precursors to the return of Trollope's disappointing sandwiches on the buffets and trolleys of our re-privatized railways, where the death knell has lately sounded over even the few remaining First Class dining cars.

Icy cold, the obligatory slice of ham, beef or chicken, hummus for vegetarians, all tasting, in spite of the 'mustard mayonnaise' and the 'fresh horseradish', of little beyond slightly rancid lettuce, lain too long with stringy tomato in plastic enveloped bread whose taste has long since dissipated. Multi-flavoured crisps, millionaire's shortbread or miserable flapjacks with eternal sell by dates; there is little excitement or enjoyment to be found amongst the gloomy packets that make up today's pre-packaged train picnics on regular services that offer only rare and expensive dining car alternatives.

For the more leisured and wealthy traveller there are exclusive gourmet train journeys; on the Blue Train in South Africa; the Wine Train in Napa Valley, California; the trains of the Orient Express company in Europe or the UK and the various 'Palaces on Wheels' in India. These provide serious restaurant food, too much and too often one sometimes hears, and a very different pleasure to the 'train meals' of the early 20th Century described by Constance Spry as 'of the nature of picnics'.

> 'I well remember the first time I had a luncheon basket on a train: ordered ahead by wire it was brought to the carriage at some main-line station en route. Now, I thought, I really am grown up, no more packets of sandwiches for me. Someone must have tipped the guard, for I remember he brought in a fresh footwarmer and inquired if I was comfortable. Hair up, long skirts, luncheon basket, the Strand Magazine, on my way to my first house party – I was beginning life. In the basket was a wing of chicken, roll, butter, biscuits, cheese and, I think, celery and possibly cake or a jam tart and an apple, and I have an idea that it cost 2s 6d, though it may have been less'.

The luncheon basket came in various guises and prices. From Chester station in 1876, 'The Aristocrat', including for 5/-, chicken, ham or tongue, bread, cheese and either a pint of claret or half a pint of sherry – followed by a cracking headache one can't help but think. 'The Democrat' offered cold meat or pie, bread and cheese with a mere pint bottle of ale or stout. In 1884 the Midland Railway provided a 'hot basket' but problems with the 'hot' description seem to have been responsible for the idea never really taking on. As dining cars on trains became more frequent and able to provide sustenance of better quality and value than the questionable contents of luncheon or tea baskets, their popularity waned, although the system only ceased altogether as food and staff shortages began to bite in 1941.

This 1912 rhyme by a railway apprentice parodying Omar Khayyam suggests that Ms Spry's memory may have had more to do with hindsight and that footwarmer than the contents of her basket.

A Loaf of Bread, a Cup of Wine, and thou
Beside me on the cushion, and I trow
The Railway train is paradise enow.

When from old age she's discline to lay,
The hen from earth is quickly called away;
Whither her Spirit goes I cannot say.

But this I know, if anyone should ask it,
Her body, or as poets say, her casket
Reposes in the Railway Luncheon Basket.

Behold the leg that wandered once at will,
With some pin feathers clinging to it still'
How thin it looks bedecked with paper frill.

The breast, unruffled now by love or care,
Looks keen and sharp when of its plumage bare;
'Twill cut your fingers if you don't take care.

Now she will quickly travel down the line,
Companioned by a bottle of bad wine,
And doubtful slice of ham, cut very fine.

And, if for further luxuries you seek,
A piece of cheese, decidedly antique,
And roll that's left the oven for a week.

Come, traveler, undo the basket's strap,
And place the savoury mess upon your lap;
You have my sympathy, my poor, dear chap.

For if upon the ancient bird you dine,
Or finish up that dose of shilling wine,
You have a keener appetite than mine.

(Dinner and the Diner - The History of Railway Catering)

A later train picnic enjoyed by Constance was, we note, made by a 'family member'. It sounds beautifully planned, quite simple but luxurious, seasonal and perfect enough for the most discerning eater at Glyndebourne or Ascot then or now.

This was for 'a small party going up to the far north':

> 'Each of us was handed when we got into our sleepers a small, neat cardboard box containing two little screw-top cartons and other small packages. In one carton was a perfectly freshly made lobster salad in a delicious dressing, the second carton contained fresh fruit salad of peaches, strawberries and orange. Crisp poppy-seed rolls were quartered and buttered, and a Porosan bag held the crisp heart of a cos lettuce. There were small cream cheese rolls made by taking two short pieces of celery, filling the hollow made when they were put together with cream cheese, and rolling the whole in brown bread and butter.'

Elizabeth David was passionate about properly made mayonnaise but not to the extent of considering it always the best sauce for a cold dish, even lobster. As she says, 'most cold lobster sauces, including mayonnaise, are on the heavy side for what is already rich and solid food'. Her sauce for 'Lobster Courchamps' is a perfect picnic dressing.

Lobster Courchamps
(Elizabeth David, An Omelette and a Glass of Wine)

'For 1 freshly boiled, medium large (about 1½lb) hen lobster or langoustine (if you are boiling the creature at home, you can always add the large goblet of Madeira called for in the original recipe), the ingredients for the sauce are 2 small shallots, a heaped teaspoon of tarragon leaves, 2 tablespoons of chpped parsley, salt, pepper, a scant teaspoon of strong yellow French mustard, 24-30 drops of soy sauce, approximately 6 tablespoons of mildly fruity Provence olive oil, the juice of half a rather small lemon, 1 teaspoon of anisette de Bordeaux.

From the split lobster extract all the red and creamy parts. Pound them in a mortar. Mix with the finely chopped shallots, tarragon and parsley. Add the seasonings and the soy sauce, then gradually stir in the olive oil, add lemon juice. Finally, the anisette.'

Cold chicken and hard boiled eggs are ubiquitous picnic foods and appear to hold a particular niche in memories of train journeys. Peter Fleming in *One's Company*, brought up no doubt with packed lunches on English trains, describes the difficulties of ordering a hard-boiled egg in sign language on the Trans-Siberian Express; a wish 'fulfilled, three quarters of an hour after it had been expressed, by the appearance of a whole roast fowl'. On a later train journey from Peking to Xian the fowl might have been more welcome than the steady diet of 'grey gruel'. By the early days of package tours to China in the late 1970s, boxed lunches provided for tourists travelling from Beijing to the Great Wall included an unshelled boiled egg with bread and butter and a banana; a similarly soothing packed lunch used to be provided on the lumbering Ilyushins of Vietnamese Airlines, a distraction from the lack of seat belts and safety drills.

As Constance Spry points out, it is essential that, to retain its freshness, your egg remains unshelled until it is to be eaten; her Porosan bags or modern cling film are poor substitutes for nature's efficient packaging. Her colleague, Rosemary Hume, remembered another train picnic of cold chicken and 'hard-boiled eggs, in their shells of course,' that included: 'French rolls with the centre scooped out, the shell buttered, and the hollow filled with a peeled and salted tomato'. With a really good seasonal tomato that sounds an excellent idea especially in days when a train picnic would have been eaten to its best advantage, at carriage temperature, not iced to soggy tastelessness in a chiller cabinet or, so fearful as we are of even the freshest foods going off the instant they are exposed to warmer air, by too many freezer packs in an insulated 'eski'.

The train picnic in *A Visit to Don Otavio*, published first in 1953 is Sybille Bedford's American, contemporaneous, story-telling version of Constance Spry's train food. I can't believe that Mrs Spry's picnics did not involve alcohol too although the pink gin may have been a more New World or colonial drink. It was certainly still being poured by the pint down the throats of the old colonial hands in the old Hong Kong clubs when I lived there – oddly accompanied by slices of white bread sprinkled with Maggi sauce. Perhaps Constance took the alcohol as a given for all readers of her books.

> 'Off at last. I got out a pint of gin, a Thermos with ice-cubes, some Angostura and from a leather case the Woolworth glasses that had long replaced the silver-bound, cut-glass mugs with which our elders travelled about a better world, and made two large pink-gins.
>
> "Did someone tip the boy from Bellows?" said E.
>
> "I didn't. Did you return the book to Mr. Holliday?"
>
> "I forgot. How awful"

"There is nothing we can do about it now". What respite, what freedom! We were in someone's anonymous and by assumption capable hands, the Great Eastern and Missouri Railroad's. There'd be four nights of it and almost four days. Four hours upright on a seat are a bore; eight damned long, twelve frightful. A difference in degree is a difference in kind: four days on a train are an armistice with life. And there is always food. I had packed a hamper and a cardboard box. Whenever I can I bring my own provisions; it keeps one independent and agreeably employed, it is cheaper and usually much better. I had got us some tins of tunny fish, a jar of smoked roe, a hunk of salami and a hunk of provolone; some rye bread, and some black bread in Cellophane that keeps. That first night we had fresh food. A chicken, roasted that afternoon at a friend's house, still gently warm; a few slices of that American wonder, Virginia ham; marble-sized, dark red tomatoes from the market stands on Second Avenue; watercress, a flute of bread, a square of cream cheese, a bag of cherries and a bottle of pink wine. It was called Lancer's Sparkling Rosé, and one ought not to be put off by the name. The wine is Portuguese and delicious. A shining, limpid wine, full almost, not growing thin and mean on one in the way of many rosés. It has the further charm of being bottled in an earthenware jug, so that once cooled it stays nicely chilled for hours. I drew the cork with my French Zigzag. The neatest sound on earth.

"Have an olive", I said.

With a silver clasp-knife I halved the tomatoes. A thread of oil from a phial, two crushed leaves of basil. "Have you seen the pepper?"'

Edmund Hull wrote in *The Anglo-Indian Vade Mecum* in 1871: 'The most objectionable feature in connection with the Indian railways is the extreme defectiveness of the refreshment arrangements'. In Indian summer temperatures the wooden predecessor to our endless insulated plastic boxes was essential to the comfort of the European traveller: filled with ice, it had a metal tray for holding food that would keep cool for a day or two while the ice melted. It was obtainable in 1907 as the 'Refrigerator (Box)' from the Army and Navy Stores in London '(packing charges extra)' for £5 5s 9d. Older Delhi friends still remember the pre-Independence May exodus to holiday houses in Simla when the Government moved lock stock and barrel to the hills. They recall with nostalgia the four berth family carriages cooled by massive blocks of ice placed in tin tubs on the floor and providing, with fans circulating the icy vapours, a primitive and much needed air cooling system. Family servants travelling in another compartment came at every station to walk the dogs, get tea or water and make the beds, but supplementary picnics brought from home of yet more cold chicken with fruit cake to follow are barely remembered in comparison with the hot food provided by the railway.

Richard Burton in *The Raj at Table* suggests that the European style picnic was superseded from the 1920s on when separate dining rooms, European, Hindu and Muslim were opened at every major station.

> 'Anybody with any sense avoided the European restaurant, except perhaps to buy a luke-warm soda or beer, for the food was as horrendous as it was over-priced. The Muslim dining rooms were quite a different story, however, and the delicious aromas of kebabs and pilaus which wafted from them proved a temptation for many a European traveller, provided they could turn a blind eye to the kitchen conditions out the back'.

The tradition of those dining rooms has continued in the unique railway food and curries that still evoke such pleasurable memories for erstwhile passengers. I have eaten Railway Mutton Curry as a special addition to a gourmet menu at a grand week-long Delhi wedding and the recipe is in *Curries and Bugles*, Jennifer Brennan's memoir of childhood and cooking in the latter days of the Raj. The food on Indian trains still arrives hot and good, delicious dal, omelettes in foil trays for breakfast, rotis, samosa, tomato soup and endless chai in the delicate clay cups that give a particular earthy flavour and, infinitely biodegradable, have been reintroduced as small weapons against the tide of indestructible plastic overwhelming the sub-continent.

Railway Lamb Curry
Serves 4-6
(Curries and Bugles)

The bones from a shoulder of lamb (or mutton); 2 inch piece of fresh ginger root; ½ teaspoon salt; 6 small red chilies, seeded and chopped; 7 cloves of garlic, smashed, peeled and chopped; 1 teaspoon cumin seeds; 2 tablespoons coriander seeds; ½ teaspoon ground turmeric; 3 tablespoons ghee; 1 large onion, peeled and finely chopped; 6 curry leaves; 1lb boned shoulder of lamb (mutton), trimmed of fat and cut into 1 inch cubes; 2 large potatoes, peeled and cut into 1 inch cubes; 6 fl oz coconut milk; 4 tablespoons tamarind liquid; 1 teaspoon salt.

Make a concentrated stock from the lamb bones, half the ginger and the salt – use enough water to cover the bones and then simmer until stock is reduced to about 8fl oz. Strain and reserve. While the stock is boiling, place the remaining ginger, the chilies and garlic in a processor or mortar and process or pound to a paste. Grind or pound the cumin and coriander seeds to a powder and add them to the paste, together with the turmeric. Add a teaspoon of water to mix the paste thoroughly. Melt the ghee in a large saucepan over medium heat and fry the onion and curry leaves, stirring constantly, until the onion is soft. Add the spice paste from the last step and stir and fry it for 3 minutes. Then pour in the stock, bring to the boil and add the meat, potatoes and coconut milk. Reduce the heat and let the curry simmer, uncovered, for at least 30 minutes, or until the lamb and potatoes are tender. The gravy should have reduced and thickened also by this time. Add the tamarind water and season with the salt. Serve with plain rice and perhaps a dhal to accompany it. The curry will taste even better if it is made the day before and re-heated.

The Indian Viceroys had their own train to take them and their vast staff on their biannual tours round the country. In 1907 there were drawbacks even to the most luxurious train travel as Lady Minto, the Vicereine, reported in her journal:

> Our journey through the Scinde desert seemed like a voyage in the infernal regions. In spite of electric fans, the thermometer was 90° in our carriages, and the whole of the dust of desert seemed to penetrate through every aperture, eyes, nose, and mouth seemed full of it, and thick layers of dust covered us from

head to foot. At meals the drinks were thoroughly iced, but the glasses felt so hot to one's lips that it was quite disagreeable touching them. The train stopped for dinner, and the windows being open, all the insects of the desert were attracted by the light. Locusts innumerable alighted on our faces and hands, springing with marvellous agility from person to person, and caused a most disagreeable diversion during our evening meal. The Staff made a large collection which would no doubt be of great value to an etymological museum. The dinner was a noisy one, many and varied screams frequently rent the air, as none of the family can be calm under the determined attack of an army of insects. The climax was reached when an enormous sort of flying frog suddenly alighted on Colonel Dunlop's shirt front. With great valour he caught the animal, in spite of a severe sting. It was hastily drowned in whiskey, and the scientists of Quetta are endeavouring to discover to what species it belongs. It was the most revolting object I have ever seen — a large scaly back, gigantic antiller, very long legs and feet composed of spreading brown coral, rather like cauliflower leaves. Had such a creature alighted on me, I doubt my still being in possession of my senses.'

On a long journey from Bombay to Trivandrum our vast insulated 48 hours worth of picnic was disdained by the children in favour of railway food and the sweets, biscuits and fruit generously and unendingly supplied by fellow passengers. Travel in India is a social affair and the hours of long train journeys spent in close proximity slip quickly by in conversation, shared food and oblivious sleep. A foreigner is always the focus of particular attention and memories of sometimes surreal conversations woven over chai and the proffered biscuit packet fuel the pens of travel writers, especially the grand master of train travel, Paul Theroux, to whom every new companion in the sleeper compartment is meat and drink.

His companion on the Rajdhani Express heading for Bombay, Mr Radia, sits reading *Blitz* magazine, the gossipy scandal sheet that feeds the Bollywood dream with gleeful reports and glossy photographs of celebrity excess.

'Mr Radia continued to read, scowling with appreciation. Then our dinner trays were brought, and I noticed his was non-vegetarian. His hamburger came apart under his knife and he poked at it disgustedly. But he ate it. "The first time I took meat I was violently sick," he said. "But that happens when you do anything for the first time, isn't it?"

With this bewildering epigraph he told me about his work. He had worked for Shell for twenty years, but discovered he loathed the English so much that he finally quit. His sense of grievance was strong and his memory for the humiliations he had been subjected to amounted to total recall. The English were domineering and exclusive, he said, but he was quick to add, "Mind you, we Indians can be the same. But the English had their chance. If only," he said, and prodded his hamburger, "if only the English had become Indians."

"Was that ever on the cards?"

"Yes, they could have done it. No trouble at all. I went to a T-group session in Darjeeeling. Debates and discussions. Very interesting. The wife of the director had just arrived from the States, and the second day she was there that lady was wearing a sari."

I was skeptical about this proving anything and asked him how long the lady would stay in her sari.

"That's a point," said Mr Radia'

Railway Biscuits
from Camp recipes for Camp People

1lb of flour, a tea cup of sugar, juice of 3 limes and the peel of half one, a large wineglassful of ghee and 6 eggs; thoroughly beat up the eggs; mix the eggs and ghee together, to which add the juice of limes and the peel; cut up small, of half of one, and stir these lightly into the flour, which will form a paste; divide it into biscuits about the size of a rupee; about a quarter of an inch thick, and bake in a brisk oven until they are a nice brown colour. with chopped parsley before serving.

Battles, Rations and Picnics in the Field

In another life my husband would have been a Napoleonic Marshall. He has an encyclopaedic knowledge of his Corsican hero, his armies and his battles. With my sons, brought up on the Sharpe novels of Bernard Cornwell, I have fought my way up the Peninsular, suffered through the battle of Salamanca and played turncoat in arguments over troop placements at Waterloo. A professionally guided tour of the Belgian battlefield was taken over by my husband before we got past the map in the visitors' centre. We stopped for our supermarket bought picnic; funny how the supermarket deli counter always seems so exciting in another country; at the surprisingly deserted remains of the Hougoumont Chateau and farm, where the Coldstream and Third Guards defended their position against an incoming tide of French attacks. As we sat in the sun by the scarred old walls we imagined the valiant red coats holding out all that long and bloody day. The fictitious Sharpe was both participant and witness at the final full stop to Napoleon's dream; the almost unimaginable slaughter of the battle summed up, when it was ended, by his companion, the great Sergeant Harper: 'God save Ireland, but we made a right bloody shit-heap of this place.'

After the battle was over, those who had survived, and they must have been surprised to live through that bloodbath, did their best to find something to eat and a means of cooking whatever they could scavenge. One officer awoke in the night from an exhausted sleep to find his men cooking cutlets over a fire in a French cuirassier's breastplate which was found to be an excellent utensil. Others used a regulation pan over a fire of lance staffs and musket butts to cook a piece of meat found in a ditch. In the slaughter house of Hougoumont, a lieutenant who had not eaten for 36 hours or more found a loaf of bread in a French haversack, from which he carefully cleaned the brain matter of another dead officer, before devouring it.

(Alessandro Barbero, *The Battle, A New History of the Battle of Waterloo*)

At Salamanca the battlefield remains much as it was in 1812 and, from the summit of the Greater Arapiles on a similarly hot summer's day the shimmering heat hazed silhouette of the old city curved into the River Tormes looks little changed in nearly 200 years. After tramping the ridges of the lesser and greater Arapiles in the footsteps of Captain Charles Synge, who left a graphic account of the battle in which he was badly wounded and left for dead, we were in a more comfortable position to beat an early retreat towards our car, The picnic of intense, chewy Serrano ham, the product of an exhaustive tasting session early that morning, with bread and bottles of light Rosado wine packed in ice, was finished off with perfect peaches.

We were eating in good company. Wellington, the villain of the piece in my husband's eyes, and the victor in a battle that was, in the longer term, the turning point in the Peninsular, also picnicked at Salamanca in advance of the battle, while his soldiers did their best to eat under enemy fire.

'The whole of the line were closely engaged ere we accomplished the business of cooking, but whenever that was effected, and the measures of beef boiled, the soup was emptied out, and the beef put into our haversacks, and we marched off the hill with the officer to join our division, which we found still lying in close-column as a reserve. Just at the moment of our arrival at the regiment, a shell was thrown by the enemy that unpiled a whole company's arms, but luckily enough, no one received any hurt. Shortly afterwards the beef was divided into messes and each man received his welcome share.'

(Private Robert Eadie, quoted in *Salamanca 1812*)

Of Lord Wellington and his interrupted lunch at Salamanca, the story has been told in several picturesque forms, varying not least in the substance of the repast. Captain Spencer Moggridge provided the following account:

He was at luncheon, and in the act of adding mustard to a slice of meat which had just been deposited on his plate, when the following colloquy took place.

'The enemy are moving, my lord,' said one of the staff officers to his commander, already busy in the office of mastication.

'Very well,' replied his lordship, 'take the glass, Somerset, and tell me what they seem to be about;' at the same time continuing his meal with every appearance of nonchalance. The officer did so for about a minute.

'I think they are extending their left, my lord.'

'The devil they are!' exclaimed Lord Wellington, springing in an instant to his feet; 'give me the glass quickly'.

(Charles Esdaile, *The Peninsular War*)

Other versions have Wellington in a farm yard surveying the French through his glass while eating a chicken leg. Seeing the French General, Marmont, duped into an ill-conceived advance, Wellington shouted 'By God, that will do!' and, tossing the chicken leg over his shoulder, mounted his horse and galloped off to command the battle.

'His cook, James Thornton, who maintained the veracity of the chicken story, was undoubtedly present, unlike other imaginative commentators. He had presumably been responsible for the cooking of the rapidly discarded bird. Thornton says that Wellington was in the farmyard less than half an hour; in general he was notorious for his lack of interest in food and his Spartan habits, carrying only a crust of bread and a hardboiled egg in his pocket for luncheon when on the march.'

Thornton's description of the cooking in camp does not suggest much in the way of gourmet pleasures:

> 'There was a mound of earth thrown up in the shape of a Balloon, and niches cut round this in which we made fires and boiled the saucepans.
> We had a larger niche cut out for roasting, we stuck a pole in the top of that, and dangled the meat, when it rained hard, they had nothing but cold meat and bread'.

(James Thornton, *Your Most Obedient Servant*)

General Alava, Wellington's Spanish liaison officer in the Peninsular came to dread the habitual answer to his query about dinner that night and the time of departure tomorrow, 'cold meat' and 'daylight'.

According to M. K. Fisher, 'Napoleon himself was a bad eater. He gobbled.'

Whether or not he actually said, *C'est la soupe qui fait le soldat* or 'An army marches on its stomach,' French soldiers have generally been better supplied than British. Their rulers and governments have understood clearly the importance of good nutrition and keeping their army happy, especially when on the move. The supply chain is of paramount importance to any military leader but Napoleon had more opportunity than most to learn from experience as his early expedition to Egypt met immediate problems when villagers fled their homes with their livestock, leaving wells blocked with stones and rubbish and the advancing soldiers to survive on biscuits, wormy from their sea voyage. Provisioning an army has been the besetting problem of all expeditionary commanders; the

Russian winter brought further disaster to Napoleon and the French army suffered hiccups in their supply lines in World War 1. British soldiers have, however, struggled more than most against apathetic, parsimonious, central regulation and vague, often unsubstantiated expectations, of paternalistic generosity towards their men from the officers of individual regiments.

Octogenarian William Henry Hare's memoir of life as a young Ensign of the 51st Regiment of Foot during the retreat to Corunna in 1808/09 suggests that officers certainly had an interest in the quality of their own victuals. Ensign Hare was also interested in his surroundings, commenting on the 'splendid garden' full of orange and lemon trees attached to the monastery in St Iago de Compostela where the officers were billeted and the 'fine old city' of Astorga, much damaged by the French. The whole army, however, was desperately short of food, lack of forage forced the destruction of most of the horses and pack mules and the chaos grew as the raggle taggle soldiery scoured the surrounding country for sustenance.

On Christmas Day in Astorga:

> 'Three brother officers and myself had clubbed together and had got a half starved turkey which we bought at the village the day before, and we bought of the woman of the house some sausages which she fried. They were tolerable excepting for the quantity of Garlic which we could not get rid of for days from our taste and smell.'

Whether Hare's memories were gilded by the glow of a happy old age, he seems determined to have seen the glass half full, finding 'very tolerable' also the men's mixture of flour and slices of fat pork (this would have been the salted pork ration in the absence of beef) cooked on the top of mess tins. A few days later as the retreat 'now became a regular rout with complete disorganization consequent on the absence of any commissariat supplies', Hare found himself cold and wet, making the best of things in a loft when he received this welcome invitation:

Picnic Crumbs

'My Dear William,
I find you are in the shed opposite me. I have got some hot soup and a bit of mutton. My brigade Major and I are just going to sit down to, and enough for you.
                                        Yours,
                                        George Cookson'
(Ensign William Henry Hare, *Archives of National Army Museum*)

It took the horrific conditions of the Crimean war and the great Reform Club chef Alexis Soyer, a Frenchman of course, to begin changes in the way army food was prepared. It was far longer before successive disinterested governments were energized to create a centralised system for the improvement of quantity and quality of rations. Part of the problem seems to have been the British soldier's own lack of care for the cooking and taste of the monotonous bully beef and bread or biscuit that would have been execrable to his French colleagues, who, as Soyer said, all 'understand a little cooking'. The soldiers ration, set in 1813 at ¾ pound meat and 1 pound of bread per day, was the same at the end of the Boer War. In 1864, years after the Crimea, the French soldiers' ration included vegetables, wine and brandy, while the British built and lost an empire fuelled mainly by tea and beer and whatever additional edibles the more enterprising could beg, borrow or steal.

In a letter written from Varna, the base for the Anglo-French force operating against the Russians at Sevastopol in the Crimea, Private John Rose of the 50th Regiment commented on the expectation of an easy victory and the abominable rations.

'We have been living on 1 pound and a half of brown bread and 1 pound of meat per day but it is not fit for men to use so some times we use it and other times we bury it'.

(Letter written by Pte John Rose, 50th Regiment, to his parents.
Varna, 28th Aug 1854).

In the aftermath of a disastrous restaurant venture after his resignation from the Reform Club, Soyer, an ebullient workaholic, was at something of a loose end. His fame was widespread and when a letter from a soldier to *The Times* in 1855 invited his advice on the cooking of rations, he was inspired to take himself to the Crimea where he started work alongside Florence Nightingale in the hospitals at Scutari. He was up against it in a situation where raw ingredients were poor to dismal and depended on the jealously guarded allowance for each soldier or group of soldiers. Cooking conditions and appliances were inefficient, dirty and unsuitable; and the army cooks and orderlies were careless and untrained. Soyer, never one to hide his light under a bushel, according to his *Culinary Campaign* changed things dramatically on his first day at work.

> 'Upon inspection I found that they had a most curious method of marking their different lots. Some used a piece of red cloth cut from an old jacket; others half a dozen buttons tied together; old knives, forks, scissors, &c., but one in particular had hit upon an idea which could not fail to meet with our entire approval. The discovery of this brilliant idea was greeted with shouts of laughter from Miss Nightingale, the doctors, and myself. It consisted in tying a pair of old snuffers to the lot.
>
> All this rubbish was daily boiled with the meat, but probably required more cooking. On telling the man with the snuffers that it was a very dirty trick to put such things in the soup, the reply was – 'How can it be dirty, sir' sure they have been boiling this last month.'
>
> When all the dinners had been served out, I perceived a large copper half full of rich broth with about three inches of fat upon it. I inquired what they did with this?
>
> 'Throw it away, sir.'
>
> Throw it away?' we all exclaimed.
>
> 'Yes, sir, it's the water in which the fresh beef has been cooked.'
>
> 'Do you call that water? I call it strong broth. Why don't you make soup of it?

'We orderlies don't like soup, sir.'
'Then you really do throw it away?'
'Yes sir; it is good for nothing.'

I took a ladle and removed a large basinful of beautiful fat, which, when cold, was better for cooking purposes than the rank butter procured from Constantinople at from ten to fifteen piastres per pound. The next day I showed the men how to make a most delicious soup with what they had before so foolishly thrown away. This method they were henceforward very glad to adopt. Not less than seventy pounds of beef had been daily boiled in this manner, and without salt. It would hardly be credited, but for its truth I can appeal to Miss Nightingale and others who were present.'

(*The Selected Soyer*)

The field-stoves Soyer invented at the behest of the Secretary of State for War, Lord Panmure, and the simple recipes he created to produce well-cooked food with the greatest fuel efficiency were adopted by the whole army at home and abroad and were still in service with the Territorial Army in the 1950s. (*A Recipe for Discontent*)

Soyer's French Beef Soup, or Pot au Feu (Camp Fashion)

Put into the kettle six pounds of beef, cut into two or three pieces, bone included; one pound of mixed green vegetables, or half a pound of preserved, in cakes; four teaspoonfuls of salt: if handy, one teaspoonful of pepper, one of sugar, and three cloves; and eight pints of water. Let it boil gently three hours; remove some of the fat, and serve. The addition of a pound and a half of bread, cut into slices, or one pound of broken biscuits, well soaked, will make a very nutritious soup. Skimming is not required.'

(Enquire Within upon Everything)

The plum pudding is solidly present in the diet of the British soldier. Elizabeth David (*Spices, Salts and Aromatics in the English Kitchen*) endorses Colonel Kenney Herbert's recommendation for 'a really good plum pudding in which a glass of brandy has been included' as a 'marvellous travelling and picnic dish', 'more welcome in the open air than ever it is on the Christmas table' (Col. Arthur Kenney Herbert, *Culinary Jottings*). I have no liking for it either way but can imagine *la recherché de temps perdu* conjured by so traditional a comfort food.

> 25th December 1915
> Dear Mother,
> As luck would have it we are still in rest for today Xmas day, but are off tomorrow. We had service in the rain here this morning, and Holy Communion afterwards indoors to which I went. Thanks awfully for the gold pin. It's a topping one. The plum puddings arrived safely and the men were awfully pleased with them. One managed to get them a pretty decent meal by buying odds and ends like beer extra vegetables etc. The cigarettes have not arrived yet which was rather a pity but managed to get them 5 each. I have put in for my leave today but don't expect I shall get it under two weeks, and that will be fairly good time, I shall get eight days I expect. No time for more now.
> Your loving Son,
Maurice

Captain Maurice Asprey was killed, aged 23, on 12th August 1916 in the Battle of the Somme.

Soyer provides an admirably straightforward field recipe for 'Cossack's Plum Pudding'.

Cossack's Plum Pudding

Put into a basin one pound of flour, three quarters of a pound of raisins (stoned, if time be allowed), three quarters of a pound of the fat of salt pork (well washed, cut into small squares, or chopped), two tablespoonfuls of sugar or treacle; and a half a pint of water; mix altogether; put into a cloth tied lightly; boil for four hours, and serve.

.If time will not admit, boil only two hours, though four are preferable. How to spoil the above:- Add anything to it.

In 1944 the inhabitants of Naples were practically starving. The great travel writer, Norman Lewis, described what it was like in *Naples '44*, the diary of his time as an intelligence officer in occupied Italy.

'Food for the Neapolitans, comes even before love, and its pursuit is equally insatiable and ingenious. They are almost as adaptable, too, as the Chinese in the matter of foodstuffs they are prepared to consume. A contact from Nola mentioned that the villages in his area had lost all their breeding storks because last year the villagers eked out shortages by eating their nestlings. This is regarded as a calamity by those who did not benefit directly, as there is a widespread and superstitious aversion in Italy, as elsewhere, to molesting storks in any way. Another example of culinary enterprise was provided by the consumption of all the tropical fish in Naples's celebrated aquarium in the days preceding liberation, no fish being spared however 'strange and specialized in its appearance and habits.'

An old friend of mine, then a very young officer fighting his way up Italy with the allies, was every bit as enterprising in the pursuit of food and as determined, too, to find the food he enjoyed. He had very clear likes and dislikes, as I well know after years of being educated about good and bad food when staying with his family while I was growing up. He would travel for miles to collect the best cheese, bread, meat, or to buy and try something new that he had heard was particularly good and should be tested. Only certain suppliers were up to the task and this must equally have been the case in wartime, judging by the diary of one of his fellow officers in 1944, even in the most makeshift field accommodation.

> 18th May: Bobs, Tony and I are living in a shelter of tarpaulin up the hill.
> Wednesday 24th May: Bobs got up at 5.30 and went to Naples before breakfast to get asparagus.'
> It is hard to imagine that the following lunch was also cooked under the tarpaulin – perhaps things had improved by then.
> 'Thursday 17th August: Roast duck and chocolate soufflé made by Bobs for lunch.

This is Marcel Boulestin's Soufflé au Chocolat. Greatly admired by Elizabeth David, his precise manner of describing food and cooking, his appreciation of good ingredients, reminds me of Bobs. He makes the soufflé sound hardy enough too, to stand up to battle zone cooking.

For this soufflé, as indeed for most soufflés, the proportion of eggs is two to each person. There are a great many mistaken ideas in connection with this delicious dish, one of them being that if you open the door of the oven it becomes flat at once; in fact a soufflé cannot be made by exact timing, and you must watch it carefully to see if it is getting on as it should be, quickly enough, yet not too quickly. Of course you must not leave the door of the oven open or open it too much, but you must not be afraid to glance at it if necessary. This chocolate soufflé is specially light, as it does not contain any flour at all.

Soufflé au Chocolat

Grate about a handful of pure cocoa, add a good deal of castor
sugar (pure cocoa is very bitter), put in six yolks of egg and melt
slowly over the fire, stirring well. See that it is sweet enough and
smooth. Put away to cool while you beat the six whites to a stiff
froth, when they are ready add them to the chocolate mixture,
put in half first and mix, then the rest and mix again. The mixing
should be done with a light hand.

Put the finished article in the soufflé dish, which you have
previously greased, with a little butter and sprinkled with sugar.

Cook and serve at once.

The war in the Western desert offered fewer possibilities for luxury
scrounging although Mike Peyton in his memoir describes one unexpected
bonus feast, a distinct improvement on the normal tinned bully beef and
hard tack biscuits with their habitual seasoning of sand.

'I've heard men say, just as they would of salt, "It needs a bit
more sand in it," and, bending down, they would take a pinch
of sand and sprinkle it in their bully stew. It wouldn't make
any noticeable difference.

It was my turn to cook and what was on offer was the normal
tins of bully or a large piece of meat. It was large because no
one else had wanted it and it wasn't difficult to see why. When
one shone a flashlight on it, it was for all the world like a huge
lump of black rubber. The inside looked as meat should, red
and bloody. There were only four of us to cook for at that time
so I could afford to waste some. When it came time to cook
this hunk of meat I sliced off all the black outer layer and cut
the rest into mouth-sized chunks and put it in the Dixie with
some tinned vegetables and left it on the Tommy Cooker while
we got on with whatever was the job in hand... What lifted it
out of the ordinary was that, just as we were going to eat it,
we got the order to move. The only thing I could do with the

now cooked meal was to fasten the lid of the billy down and wrap it up in two or three blankets to keep it warm. About four hours later when we halted and were told we were there for the night, the bundle of blankets was carefully unwrapped and we opened the Dixie. The aroma was what one would expect in a five star restaurant. As the aroma spread we could hear voices in the darkness commenting on it. We never even served it out. We simply put the Dixie on the tail board of the truck and the four of us ate carefully and quietly, keeping our spoons from chinking on the sides of the Dixie, and polished off what had been about twenty men's meat rations. It was a memorable meal. The four hours wrapped in blankets, hayboxing, had lifted what had been normal army rations into a gourmet experience.'

(*An Average War, Eighth Army to Red Army*)

Soyer would have approved.

Abroad, and Travel Food

'If you are cooking where the altitude is a factor, it will be well to keep in mind the following facts. Otherwise your results are apt to be unsatisfactory. Liquids boil at a much lower temperature so you must be prepared to increase considerably the actual cooking time to meet this condition. No great change in recipes is necessary, however, until an altitude of 2500 feet above sea level is reached.'

(Cook Away)

The 'Long Peace' of 1815-1914, the mythic Victorian Pax Britannica when Britain ruled the waves and pushed the pink of Empire across the globe, bred a domestic hunger for accounts of exploration, travel and heroism against the odds. The confidence created by relative peace in Europe and British perceptions of peaceful world domination was little dented by a mid-century hiccup in the Crimea or more distant dramas in India, Afghanistan and Africa. These indeed provided scope for an inexhaustible supply of tales of derring do and patriotic martyrdom. A new sense of adventurous possibilities encouraged travel on a grand scale as growing knowledge and improving transport began to make the world a smaller place. Journeys and expeditions were undertaken in pursuit of pleasure, ideas and the ancient civilizations whose treasures were displayed beside the fruits of industry at world fairs and exhibitions throughout the century, most notably the Great Exhibition of 1851.

These travels were the inspiration for the treasury of adventure books filling the bookcases in the old nursery at my grandfather's house. A Victorian and Edwardian treasure trove of ragged dust covers and cloth backs in faded reds and greens, deeply embossed with line drawings in coloured inks, tempting the reader to venture further in beyond the smell of dusty pages and aura of long gone publishing houses. Descriptions of Siberian exploration; the exploits of classically educated young men on suicidal quests in the Khanates of Central Asia; a married couple on a mission to pursue slavers in Egypt on a diet of plantains, sweet potatoes and the occasional hippopotamus steak; servants of Empire in the hills and jungles of India and Africa on rest and recreation hunting trips; and phlegmatic independent women in 'good thick skirts', hats firmly on their heads, accompanied by a paraphernalia of bath tubs and lace table cloths and demanding the respect of astonished natives in some of the most dangerous areas of the world.

Today's adventure seekers have dreams not so dissimilar from those earlier travellers, of new and extraordinary experiences but it is far harder to escape the madding crowd. The remaining places less travelled are mostly so for good reasons and we are seldom as little cushioned as our ancestors from deprivation and disaster. Technology and sophisticated communications make journeys easier and faster, the struggle for remarkable or unique experiences is more often supplied in ersatz form, extreme sports in extreme climates or following in the well documented footsteps of our indomitable predecessors. So far as provisioning for contemporary journeys goes, in the absence of the invaluable travel and camping appurtenances supplied by the Army and Navy Stores, we generally expect to live, if not literally off the land, locally at least. Good or bad, it will be interesting and may yet involve a hippopotamus steak. It is less likely, and more's the pity we may think, that we will enjoy the sort of grandiose picnics anywhere in the world stipulated by Mrs Beeton's disciples and spin-offs at the height of cosy Victorian self-satisfaction, or, share the tastes of early 20th century high society for ortolans or for foie gras and lobster as staples at our pastoral outings.

A travel picnic in India today is in general quite humdrum. The mundane but always welcome egg sandwich has as important a place on car journeys as the cold chicken to train travel. In pelting rain, that obscured the rhododendron-covered mountainsides of spring time Himachal Pradesh, we arrived at a deserted skiing resort, hopes of coffee and hot food fading fast. Our emergency packets of egg sandwiches were welcome padding to the scratch breakfast provided in the darkened dining room and made more interesting by the inventive insertion of spoonfuls of sugary marmalade.

On dawn jeep rides into Ranthambore national park, fingers crossed for a sight of an elusive, exquisite, tiger, the chill slowly gives way to the warmth of the rising sun as we pause at the wide view of crumbling pavilions reflected in the brightening surface of the lake. Long beaked birds dip and dive; a crocodile edges stealthily towards the drinking deer and we warm our hands on cups of spicy chai and wait expectantly as packets of egg sandwiches are unwrapped to quell early morning hunger pangs.

Travelling in Nagaland, North East India, egg sandwiches become the stuff of dreams or mirages in the face of other less recognizable eatables. Market stalls in larger towns like Mokokchung and the state capital, Kohima, display guinea pig-like rice rats, in bamboo tube cages; dog joints with all too clearly canine feet; that remarkable delicacy, hornet larvae, attached wriggling by the head in rows on bamboo pegs or stirring dozily in cubicled slabs of comb. With some relief the eye rests instead on tall ziggurat cut bamboo shoots, wrinkled red hot Naga chillis and sparkling bright vegetables, mostly destined for soggy destruction by long stewing that leaches flavour and produces dishes too dreary to eat.

Our guide, something of a gourmet with a love for Italian food, developed on one treasured European visit, craves Parmesan cheese with a hunger we come to understand well. In such surroundings, picnics are inclined to have greater curiosity value than edibility. A packet of biscuits or the solitary bag of Werther's Originals, eked out for two weeks, may be as good as it gets. Alternatives, in promising looking boxes, are cold tough stewed meat or cold fried rice; actually, not that bad if you are hungry enough and, eventually, you are. On one occasion we opened huge silver foil packages to reveal the famed delicacy of a small-town restaurant, piles of parathas that, when cold, sink like doughy boulders on our empty stomachs. I have a book of *Naga Ethnic Cuisine*, sub-titled, 'a class of its own', which it most certainly is. Most of the recipes are unsurprisingly not easily reproduceable without a supply of indigenous ingredients although I have no doubt that the inventive could swap prawns for hornets.

In Ladakh, where the Tibetan or Tibetan style local food is delicious, our picnics were disappointing. They fed the population of friendly but flea-bitten stray dogs, whose coats infested with bluebottle-sized insect life discouraged too close an acquaintance. Cooked vegetables in picnics are seldom successful; cold, in plastic bags, even the dogs thought twice before wolfing down boiled carrots and potatoes were disdained too until their tough skins had been removed. More to their taste were chocolate (flavoured I think) biscuits and, too, the egg sandwiches, over which serious animal lovers competed with hungrier and less charitable companions.

Few main roads in India are free of *dhabas* and stalls selling chai and local food at all hours of the day and night; some are to be avoided with battered foods frying in crusted *karais* and unchanged everlasting oil; others are so good as to be a goal in themselves, anticipated as a delightful interlude in a long journey and precluding the need for portable food. For me, the best food on the move in any fruit growing region of the world is the fresh seasonal fruit from roadside stalls; mangos, bananas or the scented pineapples of the North East, cut neatly with a hefty *dao*, the ubiquitous tribal knife, salted and oozing flavour. In Vietnam juicy roadside pineapples are more elegantly refined to leave a convenient lollypop-like stalk, a fiery coating of chilli powder is added with salt to shock the tastebuds with successive bursts of salty, hot and sweet.

Cowley Lambert's *Trip to Cashmere and Ladak*, the diary of a hunting and tourism journey from London in 1874, makes fascinating reading for its descriptions of local lives and landscapes and, in days when we do indeed all know about 'pushmina', for his descriptions of shawls and clothes in this beautiful and costly fabric. He finds, besides, the carpets, expensive but much to his liking, excellent cloth for hard-wearing shooting suits and gold work only spoilt by the jewellers determined use of 'Streeter's Machine-made Jewellery' catalogue as his design inspiration. Less pleasing to contemporary sensibilities are his shooting exploits, encompassing the unfortunate and rather too regular wounding of animals so rare today that we stalk them only with a camera and a lot of luck. Nonetheless 19th century sportsmen in pursuit of trophies were secure in their additional fulfilment of a suitably paternalistic responsibility to the local populace by ridding them of dangerous pests and, while a left and right of bears was a thrilling excess, Mr Lambert is a little shamefaced over the death of an old female bear whose cub escaped 'howling like a puppy', no doubt to die of starvation.

> 'There has apparently been little diminution in the numbers of black bears and their depredations cause serious injury to the crops. In 1871, four officers of one regiment carried away eighty skins, of which nearly half fell to one man's rifle. Most of the bears of Kashmir have been fired at, and near villages their temper is not of the best. The people believe that black bears sometimes carry off women into the forests, and they speak of their wonderful ingenuity – how they tie up rushes to form a shady bower, and how they sometimes tie up female bears.'

By 1895 the brown or red bears, Lambert's target, were, perhaps unsurprisingly, 'greatly diminished in numbers though still reasonably populous. The red bear is partly herbivorous and partly carnivorous and many cattle are killed every year by red bears. Length up to and slightly over seven feet.'

Lambert was more graphically interested in his prey than his stomach unlike some of his contemporaries. Nevertheless, the division of his party and their supplies into two groups was a discomfiting process and he noted the necessity of tossing a coin for a pot of marmalade against a tin of sardines among other essential and indissoluble provisions. Some solace for the loss of the marmalade, an important centre to the Victorian sportsman's breakfast, may have been forthcoming in a local gift of 'six pounds of dried apricots, which were promptly turned into excellent jam by our Khansaman'.

Bears in India are more likely to eat man than vice versa and I doubt the English hunter valued his prey for the pot although in more northern parts of the world, Alaska, Canada, Finland and the Baltic States in particular, bear meat continues to be a delicacy. No doubt the former Republican Vice-Presidential candidate, Sarah Palin, has an index full of recipes for bear meat. Internet sites for hunters abound with recipes for sausages, stews and bear meat loaf. Along with recipes for squirrel, 'cut 2 plump young squirrels into serving pieces', muskrat and groundhog, *The Gourmet Cookbook* published in New York in 1950, has several for bear, including Bear Steak Alexandre I, a recipe which, with its Worcestershire sauce and mustard, is of a very similar format to recipes for the camp food enjoyed by colonial sportsmen and other travellers.

Bear Steak

'Marinate a 41/2 pound slice of bear loin for at least 24 hours and dry it well. Rub a mashed clove of garlic on a heated platter. Make a paste of 3 tablespoons of butter, 3 tablespoons of finely minced chives, 1 generous teaspoon of mustard, 11/2 tablespoons tomato paste, and a dash of Worcestershire sauce. Cover the platter with this paste and add a thick layer of onion smothered in butter. Season with ½ teaspoon salt, pepper, and a little paprika. Keep the platter hot. Sear the steak well on both sides under a high flame and broil the meat as desired, basting frequently with melted butter. Dust the steak with salt and pepper and serve on the platter, topped with mushroom caps sautéed in brown butter and sprinkled with chopped parsley.'

The 1870s produced a wealth of travel books and stories from around the world, adding reports of less familiar and less rosy regions to descriptions of Empire life, sport, and entertainment. These accounts are the precursors to more recent travel writing, their style and humour in many cases unexpectedly contemporary and amusing.

The published journal of two years in the vast swathes of unknown territory of the Kamchatka Peninsular by the explorer, George Kennan, provides a vivid and entertaining picture of travelling life, food and his companions. He was employed by the Western Union Telegraph Company during the unsuccessful attempt to build an overland line to Europe via Alaska, the Bering Straits and the endless frozen plains of Siberia.

> '... Dodd, who never allowed his enthusiasm for the beauties of Nature to interfere with a proper regard for the welfare of his stomach, emerged from the tent, and with a mock solemn apology for interrupting my soliloquy, said that if I could bring my mind down to the contemplation of material things, he would inform me that breakfast was ready...
>
> Just as the sun peered into the valley we sat down on bear-skins around our little candle-box and ate some "selànka," or sour soup, upon which Vushine particularly prided himself, and drank tumbler after tumbler of steaming tea; "selànka", hard bread and tea, with an occasional duck roasted before the fire on a sharp stick, made up our bill of fare while camping out. Only in the settlements did we enjoy such luxuries as milk, butter, fresh bread, preserved rose-leaves, and fish pies.'
>
> (*Tent Life in Siberia*)

I do wonder how the rose leaves were eaten, whether used to flavour a preserve or jam or just as a sweet but aesthetically unappealing dark brown compost on the bread and butter. A later account of Siberian travels in the early 20th century by Fridtjof Nansen, explorer and Nobel Peace Prize winner, gives details of the recipe for *selànka*, which he describes as the national dish in Russia where soup is the invariable main dish of any dinner:

'a strong soup with pieces of the fat sturgeon floating in it; it is also flavoured with olives, capers, pickled gherkins, tomatoes and anything else of that kind. The sturgeon is eaten in the soup.'

Selànka or *solianka* is also made with meat and is the common name for something of a catch-all soup using whatever ingredients are available added to a base of onions, with pickles or lemon as souring agents and usually garnished with olives. Occasionally it is enriched with sour cream. Paul Theroux ate it for lunch at four o'clock in the morning somewhere near Irkutsk while travelling on the Trans-Siberian railway, 'a soup of fat lumps' washed down with cough mixture like port. So discombobulated was he by 'the perversity of the clocks' that he wrote in his diary, 'Despair makes me hungry'.

Mjasnaia Solianka for 6-8
(Meat soup with onions, cucumbers and tomatoes)

Put 2½ pints beef stock; 12oz lean beef; ½ lb boneless shoulder of veal, trimmed of fat and cut into ½ inch cubes, into a large, heavy casserole. Bring to the boiled over high heat, skimming off all the foam and scum with a large spoon as they rise to the surface. Then partly cover the casserole, reduce the heat to moderate and simmer for about 1½ hours, until the meat is tender enough to be easily pierced with a fork.

Meanwhile, melt 2 oz butter in a large, heavy frying-pan over a high heat. Add 6½ oz thinly sliced onions, reduce the heat to moderate and cook for about 3 to 5 minutes, until the onions are soft but not brown. Drop in 2 medium cucumbers, peeled, deseeded, halved and cut into ¼ inch slices; cook for about 10 minutes, stirring occasionally, until they are tender but still slightly firm. Then stir in 2 large, peeled, deseeded, roughly chopped tomatoes and cook an additional 10 minutes. Season with salt and a few grindings of black pepper, and transfer the contents from the frying-pan to the casserole. Add 6oz boiled ham, sliced, and 3 beef frankfurters, sliced into rounds, and simmer for about 5 minutes, until the meat is heated through.

Drop 12 stoned black olives into a saucepan of boiling water and boil briskly for 2 minutes. Drain and add them to the soup. Taste for seasoning, pour into a large tureen, and float the lemon slices on top before serving.

(The Cooking of Russia)

George Kennan continued to cast an amused and interested eye on the food provided for himself and his fellows and of the Korak people amongst whom they travelled. Their diet included a good deal of unavoidable reindeer and dog hair in the staple stew of the Siberian tribes known as *manayalla*. Made with blood, tallow, half-digested moss from the stomachs of the reindeer and dried grass for consistency, his companion Dodd, habitually cast as the comic turn, describes it as 'Like the mud pies of infancy! A little salt, pepper, and butter, and a good deal of meat and flour, with a few well-selected vegetables, would probably improve it; but it isn't particularly bad as it is.'

David Livingstone may have been the dour Scottish missionary one always imagines, albeit one in far greater sympathy with Africa and Africans than most of his contemporaries. His brother and occasional travelling companion, Charles, was thoroughly unpleasant, violent and possibly insane, but their joint account of their *Expedition to the Zambesi and its Tributaries 1858-1864* is written with a similar lightness of touch and the contemporary feel of George Kennan's journal. Whether or not it is intended or whether the image of the sick, disappointed and desiccated traveller found by Stanley puts us wrong about Livingstone, the brothers' chronicles of their travels and travails come with a distinct whiff of humour.

They had taken mulligatawny paste for soup making which was used to ill-effect by their cook.

> 'Late one afternoon, at the end of an unusually long march, we reached Mkena, near the base of Mt Niongone to the North of Zomba, and the cook was directed to use a couple of spoonfuls of the paste; but instead of doing so, he put in a whole potful. The soup tasted rather hot, but we added boiled rice to it, and, being very hungry, partook freely of it, and in consequence of the overdose, we were delayed several days in severe suffering.'

They later discovered that their illness was probably caused less by the mulligatawny, more by cassava poisoning. The sap they describe is used as a preservative in West Indian 'pepper-pot' and is called 'cassareep'. It is said to keep meat fresh, possibly for years but their cook boiled it such that the poisonous properties were improperly expelled and 'we suffered daily from its effects'.

As Scotsmen they found serious flaws in local porridge made of badly boiled *mapira* (sorghum) meal that caused heartburn. They took a serious interest in the cooking and taste of more exotic foods such as roasted 'covey' or hyrax. The hyrax, elsewhere described as coney rather than covey, is a large, guinea pig like creature, a cross-faced forager with catholic food tastes easily encompassing the rations of unwary campers. It is also, most surprisingly, a close relative of the elephant. The Livingstones ate elephant fore-foot cooked 'in native fashion'.

> 'A large hole was dug in the ground, in which a fire was made, and, when the inside was thoroughly heated, the entire foot was placed in it and covered over with hot ashes and soil; another fire was made above the whole, and kept burning all night. We had the food thus cooked for breakfast next morning and found it delicious. It is a whitish mass, slightly gelatinous, and sweet, like marrow. A long march to prevent biliousness is a wise precaution after a meal of elephant's foot'.

The brothers are pleased too, to recommend trunk and tongue of elephant, the former resembling the hump of a buffalo and the latter, as perhaps one might expect, the tongue of an ox. The rest of the beast is tough and 'from its peculiar flavor, only to be eaten by a hungry man.'

David Livingstone's fellow explorer, the passionate hunter John Hanning Speke, prided himself on his ability to live off the land, killing pregnant antelopes in order to eat the foetus. He eventually died by his own hand in what may have been an accident out shooting. His brilliant, complicated, sometime travelling companion, Sir Richard Burton, writes to him of boiled hippopotamus meat and gives a gourmet's description of crocodile eggs: 'in taste they resemble hen's eggs with perhaps a smack of custard.' (*The Search for the Source of the Nile,* Correspondence between Captain Richard Burton and Captain John Speke)

Growing British interests in Egypt during the 19th century encouraged well-heeled travellers, clutching Murray's *Handbook to Egypt*, to escape winter chills for the warmth and light of the Nile and the treasures of Upper Egypt. Frederic Eden, coincidentally Sir Anthony Eden's great uncle, voyaged up the Nile for five months in 1869, the same year the Suez Canal was opened. *The Nile Without a Dragoman* was written to rectify the deficiencies in modern practical information of Murray's guide to Egypt, more geared apparently towards the time traveller to the times of the Pharaohs. Eden intended too to reassure the economically minded of the possibility of survival without the services of the ubiquitous and expensive dragoman, a combination of courier, guide, interpreter and intermediary, a cushion between the foreigner and the foreign who could be relied upon to take a cut whenever possible.

The Edens' list of supplies brought from London is reprinted elsewhere in this book and sounds a slightly depressing form of insurance against anticipated perils and shortages in local food. They found, as it turned out, that while their large supply of mixed biscuits was useful 'backshish', their stores could largely have been dispensed with. Even Murray's ancient history *Handbook* might have suggested that olive oil was coals to Newcastle. As things were, while mourning the lack of a good Bordeaux in Cairo or Alexandria and regretting the acquisition of climatically unsuitable heavy French reds wines instead of light German whites, Frederic and his wife rapidly acquired such a taste for local coffee that they had to limit their intake while their ship's cook, Girghis, proved to be 'a most excellent baker'.

In preparation for a stay of some weeks in Nubia, a veritable farmyard of live animals was acquired as meat on the hoof. Frederic, like his sister-in-law Gertrude Jekyll, a serious gardener, must also have been a very typical Englishman in a love of animals that rapidly made the motley crew of skinny chickens and sheep into cherished pets. Their escape from the Girghis's cooking pot had continually to be engineered, even as they were fattened up like Hansel. The less appealing fowl, turkeys in particular, were sacrificed day after day to save greater favourites.

Loelia, Duchess of Westminster describes a 1931 trip up the Nile when 'The Dahabeah had a pleasant old-world atmosphere about it'. Unfortunately the food supplies were clearly a lot less well planned than the Edens'. 'We sat on basket-chairs under an awning and every few minutes shadowy figures brought us drinks. There was no refrigeration and everything went bad – the meat practically jumped off the plate and ran round the room.'

Claudia Roden's memories of Egyptian picnics are of feasts on the dunes of Agami in Alexandria where migrating quails landed exhausted on the beaches to be easily caught and then cooked on the spot. They were eaten sandwiched in pockets of Arab bread, crunched up, bones and all. The Edens' pet sheep may have ended their days roasted, in typical local fashion, whole on a spit in the open air, as Roden describes:

> Mint, sweet marjoram and garlic are all used. Push the herbs with slivers of garlic into incisions made in the meat with a sharp knife.
> The meat requires between 2½ and 4 hours (they like it well done in the Middle East but you might prefer it slightly pink inside). As it cooks, the smells conjure up the courtyards of traditional Arab houses with turquoise and cobalt blue tiles, moucharabieh (wooden lattice) at the windows and the clusters of multi-petalled jasmine with whose perfume they habitually vie. They remind me of the story my grandmother told of her childhood days in Turkey when a beggar holding two thick slices of bread was seen standing outside a pasha's yard, where the servants were roasting a lamb. When they told him to go away, he said: 'I am only soaking up the smell'.
> *(The Picnic Table)*

The diaries and journals of the servants and hangers-on of Empire, in particular the prescriptions and proscriptions for Anglo-Indian existence, include a good deal of comment and complaint about food, with picnics as 'the best amusements' (*Sleepy Sketches*). That the Memsahib's theoretical determination to produce and prefer English food whatever the cost in taste and tins, was gradually undermined by an evolutionary inclusion and enjoyment of local ingredients, is apparent in recipe books and accounts of menus, especially in camp and when travelling. Emily Eden wrote in 1839 of the food provided for her brother's camp, to the irritation of his French chef, by the King of Oude. 'Some of the dishes are very good, though too strongly spiced and perfumed for English tastes. They make up some dishes with assafoetida!* but we stick to the rice and pilaus and curries'. (*Up the Country*)

Emma Roberts, accompanying her sister and brother-in-law around India earlier in the 19th century, the 1830s, views camp food with the same optimistic pleasure and interested eye as she turns upon all aspects of Indian life in her *Scenes and Characteristics of Hindostan*. She comments favourably upon dishes invented to suit portable cooking facilities: 'A *burdwan* stew ranks high amongst these concoctions and two sauces which go under the name of *shikarree* (hunters) and camp-sauce, are assuredly the most piquant adjuncts to flesh and fowl which the genius of a gastronome has ever compounded'. For hunting parties she recommends painted snipe as a good stand in for the familiar woodcock of the north and home; jungle fowl for pheasant; rock partridge and a variety of pigeons to make 'not only an exhilarating, but a very interesting meal. The most elaborate *pic-nic* provided for a *fete champetre* in England, where people are put to all sorts of inconveniences, and must content themselves with a cold collation, is nothing to the luxurious displays of cookery performed in the open air in India.'

---

* Asafoetida was better known in Europe at the time as an ill-smelling root with medicinal properties – the French called it *merde du diable*

Two methods for Burdwan Stew

Take either cold rabbit, fowl, veal, or lamb, and having cut it into pieces, put it into a pan over a lamp, with as much good gravy as will cover it: add a piece of butter rolled in flour, an onion shred fine, two spoonsful of essence of anchovy, a glass of port wine, cayenne and salt: stew slowly for a quarter of an hour.
(The London Art of Cookery and Domestic Housekeepers' Complete Assistance)

Cut into joints a cold fowl or duck; put it into s stew-pan with half a pint of gravy, a large wine-glass of ale, half a one of white wine, the juice of half a lemon, a tea-spoonful of soy and cayenne; of mushroom catsup, lemon pickle, cucumber vinegar, corach escavecke, a dessert-spoonful each. Heat all thoroughly before serving. Cold boiled or roasted lamb or kid may be dressed in this way.
(The Practice of Cookery adapted to the business of every day life)

Hobson Jobson, the dictionary of Anglo-Indian vocabulary, throws little light on the stew. The town of Burdwan or Bardhaman, West Bengal, 67 miles north of Calcutta was, however, a district headquarters in British India and it seems reasonable to think that travellers between the two might have so named their regular camp stew.

"Our" Camp Cake
from Camp Recipes for Camp People by 'Chota Sahib'

Half a quart bottle of ghee, 1lb of flour, 8 eggs, ¾ lb of bazaar sugar (1st sort), a handful of plums, a handful of almonds, a few drops of essence of lemon and a glass of brandy; put the ghee in a basin and stir in the flour slowly; add the sugar, plums and almonds and mix these thoroughly well together; beat the eggs and add to them the brandy; add these to the cake, with a few drops of essence of lemon; keep stirring for 15 minutes, and put into a lined tin and bake thoroughly. This cake will keep good for a month.

'Chota Sahib' suggests cutlets of well-spiced pounded liver, garnished with fried parsley and a 'nice gravy' made, rather inevitably, with sherry, anchovy and Worcestershire sauce as suitable camp food. These are to be fashioned with a piece of toasted crust to imitate the bone of a chop and remind me of the delicious 'lobster cutlets' we ate as children in Scotland with a piece of macaroni serving as the fake bone.

Mrs MacNeill's
Lobster or Salmon Cutlets

Break up cooked lobster or flake salmon with fingers and add to a nice white sauce, well seasoned. Add a dash of tomato ketchup for colour and leave in frig until cold. Shape into cutlets; flour, egg and breadcrumb. Fry in hot oil and insert a piece of macaroni to imitate a cutlet bone. Serve with fried parsley and lemon quarters or with fresh tomato sauce.

Sir Francis Colchester Wemyss, author of *Pleasures of the Table*, was born a Victorian and died an Elizabethan. His interest in food was developed during his Indian army years when, like others of his fellows, his attempts to get the food he wanted to eat encouraged closer involvement in the process of its cooking. He began a two month leave pig-sticking in India in the latter years of the 19th century with less than promising provisions; by the time he and his young fellow officers had bought their horses, the only meat they could afford was a dozen tins of condemned bully beef but it sounds as if their game bag sustained them successfully as he remarks that they 'did very well living on the country'.

T. Earle Welby, author of *The Dinner Knell and Away, Dull Cookery*, not to mention a life of Swinburne and a study of the Victorian Romantics, was a journalist in India for much of his life. Elizabeth David considers his 'Shooters Sandwich' 'invaluable' for picnics and journeys.

Shooters Sandwich

Take a large, thick, excellent rump steak. Do not season it, for that would cause the juice to run out, and in grilling it keep it markedly underdone. Have ready a sandwich loaf one end of which has been cut off and an adequate portion of the contents of which has been removed. Put the steak, hot from the grill, and – but only then – somewhat highly season, into the loaf; add a few grilled mushrooms; replace the deleted end of the loaf; wrap the loaf in a double sheet of clean white blotting-paper, tie with twine both ways, superimpose a sheet of grease-proof paper, and more twine. Place a moderate weight on top, and after a while add other weights. Let the thing endure pressure for at least six hours. Do not carve it until and as each slice is required.

(Summer Cooking)

For what it is worth, a flatter loaf seems to me to be more successful with the rump steak inside, however thick it may be. Perhaps a sandwich loaf is no longer what it once was but I would rather have less loaf to more steak and in these days of multi-national bakery counters we can buy bread in any shape we choose.

When we camped in the desert in Libya with Indian friends, we too enjoyed Indian picnics and 'luxurious displays of cookery performed in the open'. The author of the *Anglo-Indian's Vade Mecum*, Edmund Hull, suggests that travelling with the 'full complement of kitchen servants' is more trouble than it is worth. We enjoyed quite enough of his pleasurable 'rough and ready living' but as our Land Cruiser lurched over ridges and valleys of endless sand we were followed by another fully loaded with the cook, his helpers and his supplies who did nothing if not add a great deal to our enjoyment. Our promised 'hotel of a thousand stars' was of course just that, an instantly created encampment of very small self-inflating tents under a great dome of darkening sky but, as dusk fell, trays of cold cans of Diet Coke were offered to us with all the ceremony of vintage Cristal as we sat on folding stools at the crest of a dune. Later, as the first stars broke the darkness, we stuffed ourselves with chicken curry and rice cooked over a fire by torchlight. In the morning our tents were surrounded by the tiny footsteps of silent night time scroungers, the original desert rats.

Leptis Magna near Tripoli is one of the great sites of the Ancient World improved upon by extensive Italian excavation and a little cosmetic rebuilding during the Italian occupation, a further bulwark to Mussolini's amour-propre and his personal mirage of a recreated Roman Empire. With Colonel Qaddafi so long persona non grata, Libya was off the tourist map for many years, allowing us the unique luxury of a whole deserted Roman city to ourselves with only wild hares for company. At tea time we watched as a human supply caravan snaked through the ruined city, shouldering cool boxes and Thermoses, to the blocks of marble where we sat overlooking the sea to eat a very English picnic of cucumber, egg, and tomato sandwiches and slices of Madeira cake while kites wheeled overhead and the fearless hares watched us calmly through the long grass.

Madhur Jaffrey and Elizabeth David have both described Indian picnics in living memory. They have very different tales to tell of eating in the gardens surrounding the Qutab Minar, the 12th century sandstone and marble tower that soars still like an inland lighthouse above a turbulent sea of dusty Delhi roads and markets. The timing of Jaffrey's childhood remembrance of the tower, surrounded by fields of mustard and millet before the concrete took over, must roughly coincide with David's adult memories. She and her unsatisfactory husband Tony David were posted in India during World War 2. Their picnic experience at the foot of the Minar was distinctly less successful than Jaffrey's family outing - David's, as she points out in *Summer Cooking*, more properly fitting into the picnic disaster category.

> 'There was nothing wrong with the transport, the food, or the moonlight; we had merely reckoned without the hordes of half-wild dogs which are a familiar feature of Indian outdoor life. Scarcely had we time to draw the cork of a bottle of the Rhinegold Australian hock which we were lucky to get in war-time India than we were surrounded by nearly every dog in the province; literally surrounded. They did not apparently

want food, or at any rate not our food; they simply formed a circle round us at a respectful distance and stared and howled.

First we pretended not to notice, then we shoo-ed them away several times. They returned immediately, with reinforcements, re-formed their dreadful circle, and howled and stared and sniffed again, until they forced us to get into our cars and return to the city, leaving them in possession of their ruin.' *(Summer Food)*

Jaffrey's picnic was an Indian scale joint family affair:

'The entire family went on the picnic. During my childhood, it did not occur to me that families could come in sizes smaller than thirty people, swelling beatifically to a few thousand at the mere hint of a wedding.'

Those 30 people piled into two cars would progress through the city and the multiple layers of Delhi history, disgorging breathless ladies in crumpled saris, tall men, servants, and all the baskets and pots of meats and potatoes, *pooris* and pickles, to be arranged on carpets and cloths while the children raced to the top of the tower:

'From the top of the tower, we children could survey all the other Delhis – the thirteenth-century Delhi of the Khilji dynasty, the fourteenth-century fort of the Tughlak dynasty, the fifteenth-century tomb of the Moghul emperor Humanun, Shah Jahan's seventeenth-century mosque, and then British India with its elegant avenues and round shopping centre.

Soon our eyes, impelled by our stomachs, would settle on something closer – the sight of a brightly edged cotton duree over which hovered some very familiar short ladies. We would think of the meatballs cooked with cumin, coriander and yohfurt and the juicy mangoes cooling in tubs of ice....and we would all come thundering down the hundreds of steps.'

(A Taste of India)

"How quick your servants are!" Miss Quested exclaimed. For a cloth had already been laid, with a vase of artificial flower in its centre, and Mahmoud Ali's butler offered them poached eggs and tea for the second time.

"I thought we would eat this before our caves, and breakfast after."

"Isn't this breakfast?"

 "This breakfast? Did you think I should treat you so strangely?" He had been warned that English people never stop eating, and that he had better nourish them every two hours until a solid meal was ready.'   (*A Passage to India*)

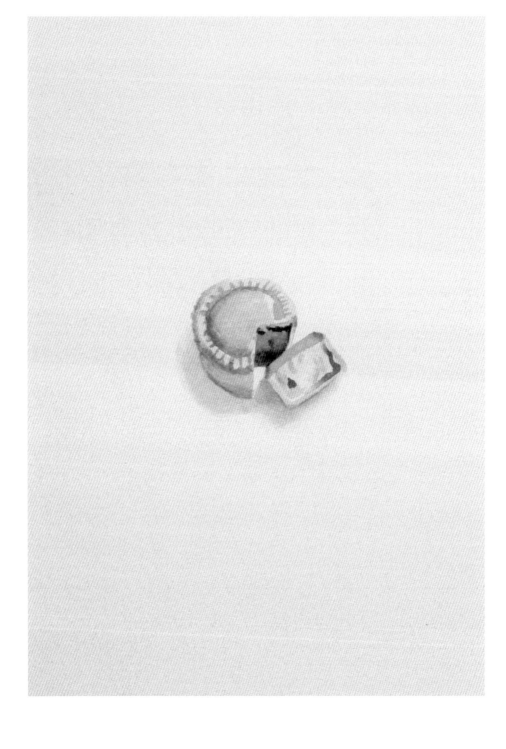

Agnes Jekyll, Hilda Leyel and other Cooks' Excursions

'Turn your thoughts to a tropical week-end in July or August, when you might expect a jaded Cabinet Minister or a depressed financier, a critic from the Foreign Office or an epicure from the Guards Club, and try them with this *Selle d'Agneau à la Miramar*. For this same festive and hot week-end remember to 'capture a stately pineapple.'

Lady Jekyll's *Kitchen Essays* were originally published in the first cookery columns in *The Times* and collected as a book in 1922. The sister-in-law of Gertrude Jekyll, the famous garden designer, Agnes was known for her remarkable skills as a housekeeper and hostess and her work for innumerable good causes for which she was duly honoured with the DBE. The essays are deliciously befrilled with aphorisms and quotations, as carefully crafted as her bowls of pot pourri and in a poetic and stylised prose that is occasionally a little indigestible for the reader.

I have no doubt that the picnic basket might make a better gastronomic and economic alternative to present day inns like the Pelican but the description of that *promenade de digestion*, its paternalistic food recycling and its potential trophies after the 'smoke of cigarette, cigar of pipe', the culmination to Agnes's '*Motor Excursion Luncheon*', certainly reduced me to tears of laughter, unlike those dry-eyed poets.

'In justice to the 'Turk's Head', it should be clearly stated that it does no more to cow and discourage travellers than many other provincial hotels in England', wrote a brilliant modern novelist lately; and a wit of the last century revenged himself for wrongs suffered by the following impromptu written in a visitors' book at departure, and no doubt equally true today:

> There stands an Inn below the hill, rightly named 'Pelican' from its enormous bill.

Similar experiences have suggested to many motorists of late that, until the innkeepers of 'this dear, dear realm of England' emulate their foreign competitors in the provision of desirable food at reasonable cost, a home-made picnic may often prove the more excellent way. Tough joints, bluish rabbit or pork pies, fly-haunted ham bones, black-eyed potatoes, cheese rocky as its birthplace in lovely Cheddar, musty biscuits, indifferent bread and butter, an atmosphere redolent of stale tobacco and beer, attendants haughty, sometimes hostile, generally indifferent until tipping-time approaches – these are not rare and isolated exceptions, but the daily fare of our long-suffering race when they take the road.

Let us, then, get out the luncheon-basket from amongst the wedding presents of a nicer age, and, in addition, contrive a small Norwegian kitchen or hay-box to hold a large screwed jar of comforting *Potage à l'écosaise* – meat, vegetables, and soup combined – a big Thermos for Mulled Claret, and a smaller one for Coffee. Slip in a couple of camp-stools and a waterproof rug as well as our furs, so that we are not tied to the car or the roadside should some sheltered nook or sunny prospect allure us. Pour a moderately good bottle of claret into a saucepan, with half the rind of a lemon, 12 cloves, a pinch of nutmeg, a tablespoonful of sugar, and let these simmer, but not boil, serving very hot. Once experienced in perfection on a cold day it will not be forgotten, and should serve to warm and unstiffen the motorists without delay, whilst the luncheon is getting itself unpacked

Finally have a nice little selection for dessert instead of pudding, made up out of the following suggestions. A small cream cheese of petit suisse wrapped in a lettuce and some crisp plain biscuits with a tiny pot of red currant jelly (the combination so popular in Duval restaurants), a box of fresh dates or pulled figs, a carton of almonds and raisins or a little screw bottle of large black French plums, or better still, a basket of fresh fruit costing what your purse can buy or your fruit room produce, a handful of glacé ginger cubes or a tin of peppermint creams, and lastly the cup of hot coffee, black or white, tasting as good out of the Thermos as tea tastes nasty. And though there is no fire, there can yet be smoke of cigarette, cigar, or pipe, to taste.

Now comes the moment for a gentle *promenade de digestion*, or stretch across open country with a motor rendezvous at the end, for enjoying the scenery of local architecture, for taking intelligent interest in Roman camp or prehistoric remains, for noting the birds and sharing your food with them, for descending, like the prophet's ravens, with the surplus of your feast, on the nearest road-menders or country children, remembering to ask their acceptance thereof with all the courtesy you can command. Perhaps before you turn homewards you will collect a few delicate trails of ivy, better taken than left, from some wayside trees, to float in your flat bowl, or a bunch of late autumn foliage or winter evergreen to gladden your town home more intimately than florists' trophies. The nursery might be made happy by a sod of growing daisies from the hedgerow, such as have given great poets thoughts too deep for tears, and which could fill the empty luncheon receptacles, only forbearing to damage wild beauty which is everybody's possession. Such a day might well hold more material comfort and bodily invigoration, more imaginative suggestion as well as some saving to sorely-tried purses, than the hours often spent in stuffy public dining rooms and crowded hotel lounges, for in the words of Meredith, 'when we let Romance go, we change the sky for a ceiling.'

(*Kitchen Essays: With Recipes and Their Occasions*)

Picnic Crumbs

A few years after the publication of *Kitchen Essays*, 'Meals Sub-Jove' received more down-to-earth treatment from the hands of a sporting gentleman, Sir Francis Colchester Wemyss. He agrees with Lady Jekyll that the best assurance of good food when travelling by car is 'a lunch basket rather than gamble on the remote chance of obtaining a reasonably respectable meal anywhere on the journey'. For solitary fishing excursions he favours food that can be transported in the pocket and eaten with one hand while playing the fish that will, sod's law, rise to your fly at your first mouthful. Piscatorial excitements notwithstanding, your sandwich will have required proper attention to its making with well-trimmed meat and, most importantly, very thinly sliced bread.

> 'The usual indigestible horror is an irregular slice of gristly meat, with a blob of mustard on one hellish corner, between two stout slabs of roughly buttered stale bread'

For winter shooting lunches Sir Francis considers the best hot dish (to be kept warm in a hay box) is a 'Pedro Pie' made in a Pedro Pie dish. Sir Francis believes that your dish with its perforated inner lid will have to be specially made. Certainly so particular an object does not appear amongst the Army and Navy's ironmongery, although there may be scope for adaptation, the potato pasty pan coming closest to the specifications. The interior of the pie is of the everything except the kitchen sink variety, a glorified shepherds or cottage pie using remains of mutton, poultry or game and every vegetable you can lay your hands on. The distinction is only in the mashed potato which is to be spread on top of the perforated lid, browned well, and cut in slices like a cake for serving with the meat mixture below. Sir Francis allows that, 'A less ambitious piece de resistance for a shooting lunch is meat turnovers'.

(The Pleasures of the Table)

Sir Francis' meat turnover might have been similar to a Cornish pasty or, more simply and economically, minced leftover meat or game inside the pastry shell. As ready-made phyllo pastry is now so easily available, I make a triangular pasty with phyllo leaves, stuffed with Chinese spiced cooked minced duck but these 'Duckling Turnovers Rouennaise' are more like something that Sir Francis might have had in his pocket.

Duckling Turnovers Rouennaise

Sift together 2½ cups flour, 1½ teaspoons salt, and a generous pinch each of powdered nutmeg, thyme, clove and juniper berries. Cut in coarsely 1 cup lard or other shortening and add enough ice-cold water to hold the dough together. Chill the dough for 30 minutes. Roll it out in a large square and cut into six small squares.

To 1½ cups coarsely chopped leftover roasted duck meat add 1 tablespoon each finely chopped parsley, chives, and onion and 1 teaspoon finely chopped green pepper. Moisten with 3 tablespoons duck gravy or rich cream sauce, highly seasoned. Put part of this mixture in the centre of each of the 6 pastry squares. Fold the turnovers envelope-fashion or into triangles. Moisten the edges of the crust with cold water and press them together. Brush with beaten egg yolk diluted in a little milk and bake in a hot oven for 12 to 15 minutes, or until the pastry is browned. Serve hot or cold.'

(*The Gourmet Cookbook*)

The provenance of the Pedro pie is mysterious, whether as a typical shooting lunch dish or for any other occasion, in or outdoors. A 'Don Pedro pie' appears in a memoir by Nathaniel Beard. His father was doctor to Wilkie Collins, author of *The Moonstone* and *The Woman in White*, opium addict and lover of food and wine. Amongst all the vegetable variety of Sir Francis' pie recipe garlic is singularly absent.

> 'One evening Wilkie and my father had talked themselves into quite a culinary fever over a certain "Don Pedro pie", which the former had recently tasted during his travels. At last they arranged that the thing should be put to tangible proof. The next day, the materials having been procured for this delicacy, Wilkie came round, and he and my father went solemnly into the kitchen together, each adorned with an apron which had been borrowed from the cook, and instructing, pointing out,

and occasionally joining with the cook in the practical details of the manufacture of the much-praised dish. Then they returned to the upper regions, flushed but victorious, and the dish was the dinner — or the main feature of it — for the evening. It was a glorious success, but there was just one little drawback. The garlic had predominated so strongly that no one save the two *chefs* themselves could venture upon tasting it. The upshot of it all was that Wilkie went home and took to his bed, while my father remained at home and took to his. They were both very ill for several days, with a horrible gastric attack, and garlic was never more mentioned in the house.'*

While the extravagantly themed parties, given by the great hostesses and decorators like Syrie Maugham and Elsie de Wolfe, continued during the 1930s, the hyperbole of society cookery books reduced. In descriptions of food for travelling in particular, Lady Jekyll's fantastic picnic directives and Hilda Leyel's marvellously inventive recipes from *The Gentle Art of Cookery* gave way to suitably practical suggestions in her 1936 *Picnics for Motorists*. The gathering clouds of austerity still allowed for a foie gras pie but her note that it is both expensive and ambitious discourages; the inclusion of a pound of truffles makes it sound impossibly sybaritic today.

Mrs Leyel recommends the 'wide mouthed thermos flask' for curries and soups both hot and cold but her statement that 'The art of arranging cold meals is to choose dishes that are better cold than they would be hot' is somewhat belied by several recipes that could not possibly be so. I am unconvinced by a 'Cold Liver Loaf' or cold 'Excellent Fish Pie', a sort of kedgeree under a pastry crust, even with a salsa-like uncooked 'cold catsup'. Cold pheasant is fine if usually dry and one can't help feeling that the opening of a pot of cold bread sauce to help it down is unlikely to be met with cries of joy. Elizabeth David, for whom Mrs Leyel was an early inspiration, did not, unlike her, favour dishes in aspic, melting away on a warm day. Some of the recipes would undoubtedly do better indoors but there are plenty of transportable and unusual salads and soups,

---

* Nathaniel Thomas Beard was the younger son of Francis Carr Beard, Wilkie's doctor and friend for much of his life. Nathaniel Beard was later chief clerk at Bentley's publishing house. Beard's *Some Recollections of Yesterday* published in the periodical *Temple Bar* in 1894 includes six pages of childhood memories of Collins' visits to the family home at 44 Welbeck St.

and a chocolate mousse, if improbable picnic food, is always going to be acceptable if it survives the journey.

I like horseradish and Mrs Leyel likes it in her salad dressings which make very ordinary ingredients a lot more interesting. She grates it over a green pea and ham salad, otherwise dressed simply with oil and vinegar and uses the cooked salad dressing for this pea and potato salad and another of beetroot and celery.

Horseradish, Pea and Potato Salad

Choose waxy potatotes, cook them and chop them into small pieces; cook some green peas and let them drain well, and freely shred a stick or more of horseradish.

Then put the peas and potato into a salad bowl and mix the horseradish with it. Cover with the following sauce:

Beat two eggs in a double saucepan, add a saltspoonful of salt, a teaspoonful of mixed mustard, two dessertspoonsful of sugar, an ounce of butter, four tablespoonfuls of milk and three tablespoonfuls of vinegar.

Stir until thick and then pour over the salad.

Elizabeth David's own memory of a pre World War 2 picnic with American acquaintances while visiting friends in France is a story of dashed expectations.

'It was agreed that the two parties should proceed in their own cars to a little bay outside Marseille, and that we should each bring our own provisions. On Sunday morning I and my friends indulged in a delicious hour of shopping in the wonderful market of the rue de Rome, buying olives, anchovies, salame sausages, pâtés, yards of bread, smoked fish, fruit and cheese. With a provision of cheap red wine we bundled the food into the car and set off, stopping now and again for a drink; so that we arrived at our rendezvous well disposed to appreciate the sun, the sea and the scent of wild herbs and Mediterranean pines. Presently our friends drove up and started to unload their car. One of the first things to come out was a hatchet, with which they efficiently proceeded to chop down olive branches, and in no time at all there was a blazing fire. Out of their baskets came cutlets, potatoes, bacon, skewers, frying pans, jars of ice, butter, tablecloths, all the trappings of a minor barbecue. Our reactions as we watched these proceedings were those of astonishment, admiration, and finally, as realization of the inadequacy of our own catering dawned, dismay. How wilted they seemed, those little packets wrapped up in rather oily paper; the olives which had glowed with colour in the market stalls of the Rue de Rome looked shabby now; the salame seemed dried up and the anchovies a squalid mess. Miserably, like poor relations, we sat with our shameful bundles spread out on the grass and politely offered them to our friends. They were kind, but obviously preferred their own grilled cutlets and fried potatoes, and we were too embarrassed to accept their proffered hospitality. Presently they produced ice cream our of a thermos, but by now we were past caring, and finally it was their turn for surprise when they found we hadn't even provided ourselves with the means of making a cup of coffee.'

(Elizabeth David, *Summer Cooking*)

Arabella Boxer, Marian McNeill and Claudia Roden are all advocates of outdoor cooking, McNeill and Roden both providing much practical advice as to cooking equipment, method, invention and tradition.

'To get back for a time to primitive ways of living and to close contact with the soil from which we have sprung - that is one of the best prophylactics against all the ills that flesh or spirit is heir to. Sometimes it is a call of the blood, sometimes an affinity of spirit, and sometimes merely the desire for a change of scene that determines whether we shall pitch our tent among the lush meadows and limpid streams of the south, or close to some dark pine forest and tumbling waterfall in the north, or, again, on the green machair, within sound of breaking waves, on some western isle. But, wherever we go, we should live not only *on* the land, but as far as possible, *off* it. This is the first rule for the camper's kitchen. And beyond that there must be a cook: 'We may live without friends, we may live without books, but civilised man cannot live without cooks.'

(Marian McNeil, *The Camper's Kitchen*)

'I am convinced that the nicest barbecues are home-made, whether a permanent feature in a corner of the garden or terrace or a temporary construction on the beach or camping site. These also solve the storage problem since many commercial barbecues take up as much space to store as a lawn mower. Simple cast-iron grills can be bought, for laying on a base made with bricks. Sandwich-shaped wire grills with long handles are also available, for holding food while grilling. Fish-shaped wire baskets in various sizes can be found; small ones are useful for holding trout or small red mullet, while large ones hold bass or grey mullet, and stand on their own legs directly over the coals. When barbecuing, care must always be taken to prevent the food becoming burned. If this threatens, it should be moved slightly farther from the heat than usual and watched like a hawk.'

(Arabella Boxer, *The Vogue Summer Cookbook*)

In *South Wind Through the Kitchen*, the 1997 anthology of Elizabeth David's work, her friend April Boyes wrote: 'All of Elizabeth's friends have stories to tell about her picnics which ranged between disaster and triumph.' When Elizabeth was researching a book in the Guildhall Library in 1974, picnics in a nearby square were the order for lunch throughout the summer. Not surprisingly they sound quite delicious; a tian, home-made bread, cheese, and the all important wine. The bottle was attached with string to a convenient bush and lowered into the central pool in the square to cool during the morning's work. Amazingly it never got stolen.

Elizabeth David was inspired by Hilda Leyel who considered wine a most important adjunct to food.

> 'Nowadays, when French wine is to be had for two shilling a bottle, it is a pity that the northern nations do not emulate the southern races and drink more wine. The light wines of France or Spain are more wholesome than spirits or than the strangely concocted cocktails with weird names that come from America.
>
> Why is it that drinking is so much more poetical than eating? Homer wrote lyrically about "sweet honey-hearted wine," but the rebuke of Antinous to Odysseus, whom he accuses of being "wounded with the honey-sweet wine" that "taken in great draughts and drunk out of measure darkened the mind and the heart of Eurytion, so that he wrought foul deed and began the war between the Centaurs and manking," is far more poetical than any modern temperance literature, and no less convincing.'

(Elizabeth Kent quotes the *Girl's Own Paper* in her book *Picnic Basket;* the Claret Cup recipe is Mrs Leyel's)

Claret Cup

Wrap the ice in a blanket and put it under the seat of the wagon. Claret cup is sure to be wanted, to be mixed on the spot by one of the men of the party. I have noticed that when a man has made a claret cup which is appreciated he feels thoroughly satisfied and at peace with the world in general.

Put into a bowl the very thin rind of a lemon, a little sugar, and a wineglassful of sherry. Add a bottle of claret, sugar to taste, a spring of lemon-scented verbena, one bottle of aerated water, and a grated nutmeg. Strain and ice. (A whole grated nutmeg is a lot for one bottle only of claret – it is safer to grate and taste as you go along)

Social Graces and Summer Seasons

'The word "Edwardian" merely calls to mind a picture of ladies having tea on the lawn. It is a lovely sunny afternoon and there are no midges and only an occasional wasp; menservants carry out creaking basket-chairs made comfortable with fitted squabs and frilly cushions and a folding table and white embroidered table-cloth and a silver tea-tray on which is a silver tea-equipage and a silver instrument like a hunting horn for extinguishing the flame under the kettle when tea is over. There is pretty floral china and plenty to eat – very thin slices of bread and butter, hot scones, cucumber sandwiches, a virgin seed cake, sugar cakes, home-made biscuits and iced coffee. The ladies have elaborate hats and parasols and gloves – they are determined to defend themselves against the horrors of sunburn – and they stare at the children through lorgnettes – rather rude the children think – and they all seem exceedingly glad to see each other and amused by each other's remarks.'

(Loelia, Duchess of Westminster, *Grace and Favour*)[*]

The padding on the bones of the summer social seasons we know from Victorian and Edwardian novels and memoirs is as long gone as those ladies and their lorgnettes, but the skeleton of sporting events, the Derby, Royal Ascot, Wimbledon or Henley Regatta, maintains for a

---

[*] Loelia Westminster's memoir might be expected only to be full of the social round she experienced first as the child of a courtier, a debutante, and then wife of the fabulously rich Bendor Westminster. Surprisingly, among other equally down to earth memories, she notes that during the war her great friend Diana Cooper taught her to make Pont L'Eveque cheese – at the least, an unusual accomplishment. (*Cocktails and Laughter*, Hamish Hamilton, London, 1983)

larger and more democratic audience. Monuments of earlier seasons like the Eton Harrow cricket match still continue but without the social hullabaloo of the past. More recent additions to the summer round, the opera at Glyndebourne, founded in 1934, and its more recent imitators, have added to the number of excuses for latter day Fête champêtres and contemporary picnic one-upmanship. Things got out of hand a few years ago at the 4th of June at Eton, the historical celebration of George III's birthday and a day when parents and their sons picnic on the sports fields. The past high society connotations of a private school event were revived as the exclusive bait for corporate entertaining by opportunist outsiders with marquees, an innovation unsurprisingly deplored by the headmaster. The headmaster at my sons' old style preparatory school was outraged when a misguided parent appeared on Sports Day with a small tent and a large barbecue; typical picnic food on rugs on the cricket pitch followed by a spectacular school tea were the proper and expected order of the day.

The committed sportsperson may always have had reservations about turning an important event into a social occasion. Alfred E. T. Watson, in a 1903 critique of Henley as a venue for international competition, comments: '- the course is not suited for it. In the first place it is too short; in the second place it is too crowded with pleasure boats, and, if I may use the word, is too picnicky.' (Alfred Edward Thomas Watson, *English Sport*)

The sport versus picnic problem has not improved in these days when no one can survive a short walk without bottles of mineral water and/or additional sustenance. In June 2009, the following letter appeared in the *Daily Telegraph* from disgruntled of St Leonards-on-Sea:

> 'While trying to enjoy a day out at the Centre Court at Wimbledon this week, we were continuously disrupted by so-called tennis fans rustling plastic bags, opening food containers and chewing, gulping and occasionally burping while indulging in their culinary delights.
>
> I had always assumed that the Wimbledon courts were an arena to watch tennis and not a place to have an afternoon picnic.

> The Lawn Tennis Association should prohibit the annoying
> and distracting consumption of food within the main courts.
> There are numerous areas in the grounds to enjoy a picnic.
> After all, the players demand a quiet environment while
> playing, so why can't the spectators while watching.'

At the Queen's tournament this year, the noise from surrounding eaters was less of a problem than the sight, why do other people's packed lunches look so dissimilar to anything one would wish to eat oneself? Years ago when the international tennis tournament in Hong Kong was one of the major occasions of the year we used to have quite silent and, I hope, reasonably elegant picnics; tiny cucumber, ham or tomato sandwiches; very good white wine, admittedly in paper cups – light weight and no clinking; and flasks of deliciously flavoured consommé, drunk from the same disposable vessels.

These days most entertainment and sporting venues bustle with food outlets and the proper picnic, as opposed to the impromptu audience snack, may seem too much time, trouble, and too reliant on unpredictable weather. The social picnic, where it does happen, may be at least as competitive as the event in hand, whether for its home made perfection or as a demonstration of money-no-object professional catering. Remembering shivering over the sandwiches in a drizzly car park at Royal Ascot, I have complete sympathy with those who think the effort versus pleasure ratio unequal; at the same time, an interval picnic in the gardens at Glyndebourne on a beautiful evening remains one of the great pleasures of an English summer.

This description of a 19th century Goodwood Cup Day at the summer Goodwood race meeting, the traditional end of the social Season, sounds horribly familiar:

> A couple of races of no great importance are run, races with
> which social Goodwood, unless friends own competitors, have
> little to do. Luncheon time is coming, and with many anxious
> glances upwards from kindly hosts and hostesses, to say
> nothing of hungry guests, parties are arranging themselves

round hospitable tablecloths. If on the beech leaves overhead the raindrops should begin to patter down, lunch is of course ruined. Into the champagne glasses they drip, and by no means improve the delicate flavour of the '74 Perrier Jouet; the Mayonnaise presently assumes a spotty appearance. Leaves fall from the flowers which tasteful luxury provides in water glasses as at a dinner-table; a moisture not its own is given to the pigeon pie; and a sort of rain gravy forms in dishes of cold chicken; ladies pull up the hoods of their ulsters, men turn up their collars, umbrellas spring up all down the beeches like a growth of magical mushrooms.

(Alfred Edward Thomas Watson, Racecourse and Covert Side)

Judging by the memories of Glyndebourne kept in its archives, picnics there have always been variable feasts although champagne has a regular role. Wonderful though these alfresco dinners may be, there is no doubt that it is easier to eat, safe from the elements, in the restaurants but it does rather take away the romance.

SUMMER 1958

I was a young fellow working in London, and I had two tickets in the Gods, bought months in advance, for My Fair Lady. My flat-mate at the time was seriously courting a young woman whose father owned several thousand acres of East Anglia, and who was desperate to see My Fair Lady.
'All right,' I said finally, 'you can have my tickets, but in return I want two tickets for Glyndebourne.'
'Done,' he said.
Working in Baker Street at the time, I flogged along at lunch time to Ibbs and Tillet, who ran Glyndebourne's London box office. They offered me two stall tickets for Le Comte Ory which set me back six pounds the pair (twice the price of my Drury Lane tickets).

In those days, when one only had two weeks holiday a year, the next problem was to find someone with whom I could escape from London for a few hours on a midweek afternoon. I remembered Jenny.

Jenny was a model with gorgeous red hair, and, yes, she would love to come. She had heard of Glyndebourne, which was rather unusual in those days amongst the girls I usually went out with, but, like me had never been there. I told her we would take a picnic – I would bring champagne and she volunteered to bring the food.

Came the interval and we returned to the car park to collect our picnic. On the way back I saw Jenny looking at some of the picnic rugs on which smoked salmon and asparagus were appearing.

'I'm afraid,' she said apologetically as she produced a brown paper bag from her shopping basket.

'Looks lovely,' I said, wondering what it contained. 'Let's find somewhere to sit."

I think we ended up by the lake, though, after fifty years, it's hard to be sure. I dug out the champagne, popped the cork and filled our glasses. Meanwhile Jenny busied herself with her brown bag, which contained a packet neatly wrapped in grease proof paper.

'I'm sorry,' she began again. 'I had no idea it was like this – '

'Please,' I reassured her. I raised my glass to her.

Slowly she unwrapped the grease proof paper and exposed four tomato sandwiches. How we laughed. Champagne and tomato sandwiches!

(Anon. Glyndebourne)

Arabella Boxer, the author of the famous *First Slice your Cookbook* (a book where each page is cut horizontally into three for easy assembly of different menus that can be viewed in one spread), understands from longer experience what is expected of a Glyndebourne picnic.

'A totally different sort of picnic that occurs, though less frequently, in my life is the evening picnic. An expedition to Glyndebourne is a good example of this sort of occasion, and here it seems worthwhile to be more extravagant. I like to construct this sort of picnic as if it were a formal meal, served on china plates with proper silver and glass, taking a pretty tablecloth to spread on the grass. Several bottles of chilled white wine, or even better, still champagne, are almost obligatory. To start, perhaps home-made potted shrimps with small sandwiches of brown bread and butter, or giant prawns or crayfish, served with mayonnaise. The possibly some small chicken pies, served warm; or a roll of flaky pastry enclosing a large spicy sausage served with a mustard sauce; or an enclosed quiche, like a shallow pie, filled with spinach and tomatoes, or mushrooms, fish and rice. An alternative menu might consist of a hot consommé madrilène or a bortsch served in small cups and followed by a cold main dish such as smoked chicken or turkey, cold duck, or a duck pâté with crusty French bread and a green salad. Slices of cold roast sirloin can be rolled round small heaps of freshly grated horseradish, or thick slices of rare fillet of beef can be served with a rich and creamy horseradish sauce.'

She recommends a tin of chocolate brownies as an easy pudding.

It sounds delicious, if the rain stays away. Dozing off after a good dinner and 'several bottles of white wine', not to mention pre-performance Pimms, is another hazard although the latest, air-conditioned theatre at Glyndebourne has reduced the problem. In the old, cramped and close space, programmes swished constantly in a vain effort to stir the air. One man had a heart attack in the front row and was quietly removed as the music played on and a woman in a daffodil yellow dress crumpled to the floor during the interval cutting her head on the stone steps.

I am never convinced about home-made potted shrimps given the general taste for the bought variety but the idea is appealing and more so now you can buy plastic boxes of fresh shelled brown shrimps. Shelling them yourself is a thoroughly unrewarding chore and larger shrimps just aren't the same.

Arabella Boxer's potted shrimps

- 360g shelled cooked shrimps
- 240g butter
- ½ bay leaf
- Pinch of gound mace
- Coarsely ground black pepper

Cut the butter in pieces and melt it. Add the bay leaf and mace and leave for 5 minutes. Add the shrimps and some freshly ground black pepper. Stir gently and then cook for 10 minutes, stirring now and then. Spoon into one dish or small individual ramekins, covering the shrimps with the seasoned butter. They will keep for two weeks in the refrigerator.

(The Vogue Summer Cookbook)

Leith's caterers are now in charge of the restaurants at Glyndebourne for those who wish to play safe with the weather. For inveterate and wealthy picnickers the various options come at a cost of around £58 per head with a half bottle of champagne per couple or £48.50 with white wine plus a variety of possible luxury supplements. These days, if it is wet, there are tents available for sheltering picnickers, although it does rather take the edge off things nonetheless.

If it is true that £1 in 1907 is equivalent to about £85 a century later, Leith's champagne menu, without supplements, is only slightly more expensive than the flat rate of £8..14 shillings and threepence for a hamper for 12, 'suitable for Races, Picnics, Regattas &c', from the Army & Navy Stores in 1907. The 1907 version is, however, a good deal more generous with the drink. It contained 'Boiled Salmon or Lobsters, Pigeon Pie, Roast Fowls, Ham, Rolled Tongue, Salad and Dressing, Mayonnaise Sauce, Bread, Rolls, Butter, Cheese, Cake, Pastry & Condiments' then a bottle of Achille Morat Champagne per head plus 2 bottles of Sherry, 4 of Claret and 1 of Whisky or Brandy'. Linen, plate, glass, cutlery are all included.

Starters

Asparagus vinaigrette **V**

Smoked salmon and caper berries

Goat's cheese panacotta

Tian of crayfish tails, apple frisée with roast garlic aioli
(Supplement of £4.50)

Chicken liver parfait and quince jelly

Ham terrine with mustard pickle

Cèpe & Taleggio tart **V**

Main Courses

Rare fillet of beef with horseradish sauce

Whole lobster salad **(Supplement of £9.50)**

Poached Scottish salmon fillets with lemon and black pepper

Gressingham duck, sesame seed, mange tout salad & citrus dressing

Trout and pear stack with rocket, watercress and endive

Tomato & spinach celeriac roulade **V**

Puddings & Cheese

English strawberries and cream

Tropical fruit salad **V**

Summer pudding

Chocolate truffe

Lemon tart with crème fraîche

Selection of British cheese **V**

Coffee & Chocolates

PORTER SERVICE

Porter Service for parties of up to 8 persons (Supplement of £25.00)
Above 8 persons - supplement per extra cover (Supplement of £4.00)

FURNITURE

Picnic tables (Supplement of £15.00)
Picnic chairs (Supplement of £6.00)

The best known predecessors of contemporary society picnic dinners, not to mention expensive catering arrangements, are the suppers and refreshments once to be had in the Vauxhall Pleasure Gardens. At their peak during the late 17th and 18th centuries the Gardens were the place to see and be seen although much of the entertainment available was a good deal bawdier than that provided at Glyndebourne. There were over a hundred decorated supper boxes, with seating for six to eight people, in which very small quantities of food were offered at considerable cost. A dish of wafer thin ham cost one shilling and it was said that the Vauxhall carver could cover the whole Gardens with a single joint. By 1817 a minute portion of ham with two chickens cost 11 shillings, biscuits and cheese cakes another 4s..6d and a quart of arrack, 7s. The wines were reputedly excellent and the arrack, made from rum and grains of the medicinal benjamin flower, famously intoxicating.*

> 'These Flowers are, without doubt, the most essential Part of the Benjamin, whose principal Virtues are as well to subtilize bad Humours and expel them through the Pores of the Skin, as to loosen and expel the thick and viscous by the ordinary Ways, chiefly those of the Breast and Lungs: Dose from three Grains to ten in any proper Liquor. They are profitable in vehement Catarrhs, Coughs, Colds, Asthma's, and Obstructions of the Lungs; procure Sweat excellently in venereal Cases, given in a Decoction of Guajacum, and fortify a weak Stomach.'
>
> (Pierre Pomet, *A Complete History of Druggs* 1709)

---

* The benjamin bush, otherwise known as feverbush or spice bush, provided a herbal remedy for colds, dysentery and intestinal parasites and is still used today in Chinese medicine.

An Apophlegmatic Lohoch

Take Syrup of Hyssop 2 ounces and a half; Oil of sweet Almonds 1
ounce; Oil of Anniseed 2 drops; Tincture of Myrrh 1 dram; powder'd
Orris root 4 scruples; Flower of Benjamin half a scruple; Tobacco 4
grains, mix.

By pricking the Parts, drawing the limpid Saliva, inciding thick
Phlegm exonerating the Glands, and lubricating the Passages. It
brings viscid Phlegm up out of the Throat, and is useful whensoever
the Uvula, Parotides, and internal Parts of the Gula are swell'd,
and oppress'd with mucous Filth: And when the Secretion is to be
provok'd, and a failing Cough to be recover'd.

(Fuller, Pharmacopoeia Extemporanea)

Taking your own dinner or at least a hand in the cooking of it may have
made for a more generous dinner than that provided by the carver but the
diarist Horace Walpole makes it sound a somewhat haphazard affair.

> 'At last we assembled in our booth, Lady Caroline in the front,
> with the visor of her hat erect, and looking gloriously jolly and
> handsome. She had fetched my brother Orford from the next
> box, where he was enjoying himself with his petite partie, to
> help us to mince chickens. We minced seven chickens into
> a china dish, which Lady Caroline stewed over a lamp with
> three pats of butter and a flagon of water, stirring and rattling,
> and laughing, and we every minute expecting to have the
> dish fly about our ears. She brought Betty, the fruit-girl, with
> hampers of strawberries and cherries from Roger's, and made
> her wait upon us, and then made her sup by us at a little table.'
> (Horace Walpole, *Letters, Vol. II*)

In *The Citizen of the World,* Oliver Goldsmith's Chinese philosopher is
invited to the Gardens with friends where: 'The widow found the supper
excellent, but Mrs Tibbs thought everything detestable: "Come, come, my
dear," cries the husband, by way of consolation, " to be sure we can't find

such dressing here as we have at Lord Crump's or Lady Crimp's; but for Vauxhall dressing it is pretty good: it is not their victuals indeed I find fault with, but their wine; "their wine," cries he, drinking off a glass, "indeed is most abominable"'.

The Gardens finally closed in 1859 but by 1821 Eden Pierce was describing the 'refreshments to be of the best quality, and supplied upon moderate terms', a transformation that may have led to the bankruptcy of the owner in 1839.

> 'Now is the cheerful white-covered table set, and decked with polished utensils. The juicy fruits of the hot-house, hyacinthine Xeres in crystal cups, and champagne covered with thick mist, from the ice, await the guests.'
>
> (Pückler-Muskau, *Tours in England*)

As roads and coaches improved during the 18th century, society increasingly decamped to the great country houses for entertainments that whisked them from the ballrooms, down sweeping stone staircases and out into landscaped gardens and parks, ornamented with follies, grottoes and temples. Those at Eaton Hall, Loelia Westminster's sometime home, did not impress the traveller and garden designer Prince Hermann von Pückler-Muskau on a visit in the 1830s. 'A number of 'affreux' little Gothic temples, deface the pleasure-ground, which has, moreover, no fine trees: the soil is not very favourable, and the whole seems laid out in comparatively recent times. The country is rather pretty, though not picturesque, and too flat.'

A new interest in country life and rustic living among the upper classes encouraged the inclusion of estate workers and locals in outdoor entertainment and feasting on a spectacular scale. The 'peasants' were not, it seems, always present solely for their own pleasure.

> 'Yesterday, the wedding day of the Duchess of St. A, was celebrated by a very pleasant rural fete at her villa. In the middle of the bowling-green was a Maypole decorated with garlands and ribands, and gaily-dressed peasants in the old English costume danced around it. The company wandered about in

the house and garden as they liked; many shot with bows and arrows; others danced under tents, swung, or played all sorts of games, or wandered in the shade of thick shrubberies; till at five o'clock a few blasts of a trumpet announced a splendid breakfast, at which all the delicacies and costly viands that luxury could furnish, were served in the greatest profusion.'

The ice cream named in honour of Pückler-Muskau, Fürst Puckler Eis, is a form of Neapolitan which those with a sweet tooth and a taste for colour may enjoy. The original was probably more of a layered iced dessert than the multi-coloured ice cream which is traditionally served sliced, with each slice coated in chocolate sauce and arranged on a plate garnished with whipped cream.

The Review of the Hertfordshire Volunteers and Militia at Hatfield House, home of the Earls of Salisbury, in 1800 was a stupendous feat of conspicuous consumption, attended by the temporarily sane King George III, and other members of the royal family. Estate entertainments to celebrate comings of age or birthdays of landowners or their heirs have continued on great estates to the present day although on a reducing scale in the last hundred years or so.

At Hatfield 25 tables of 25 were set outside the house with one bottle of port per two people; butts of ale and small beer placed 'in different directions' and reserves of wine in case of need. 'The quantity drunk that day in the Park, Tents and House, exceeded 1300 bottles of wine, of various sorts' while some idea of the food is suggested by the list which was 'part of it' and included; 120 pieces of boiled beef; 104 quarters of lamb; 96 pieces of roast beef; 110 joints of veal; 70 hams; 60 meat pies &c; 70 tongues.

> 'In the afternoon of the next day, the remnants were distributed to nearly one thousand persons, exclusive of joints which were clandestinely carried off the evening before.'

The King and the Royal Family had retired indoors to a dinner served in two courses that included:

Voulouvan aux canuffes; Haunch of venison; Grenades de Veau; Pâté de macaroni; Gateau de Savoie; Corbeille de patisserie; Goose roti; Crayfish; and Orange jelly. There was a side table of cold meats, and desert, chiefly of 'forced fruits and ices'. 'Their Majesties after dinner drank coffee and tea in the library', of which one imagines they were much in need. (*Narrative of the Preparations at Hatfield House for the Review of the Volunteer Corps and Militia, 13th June 1800*)

Provisions

'Certain articles which can now be purchased in tins and bottles are so perfectly done that – granted a good cook – it is absolutely impossible to tell the difference between them and fresh. To mention a few at random we would say mushrooms, white currants, raspberries (the Café Grand, Karachi, have some very excellent raspberries in tins which have the great merit of each raspberry being whole), celery, larks in foie gras and strawberries in brandy. None of these can be produced fresh in Sind and therefore if one desires any of them to complete a recherché dinner, it is necessary to obtain them in tins or bottles. Any of the last mentioned items can be obtained from the Army and Navy Stores, London, or Harrods and if ordered direct, are very cheap even including freight and customs duty.'

(*CC Lewis, Culinary Notes for Sind,* quoted in *Curries and Bugles,*
Jennifer Brennan)

'There is a creature something like a whale, for he lives in the cold northern waters as whales often do, and something like an elephant, for he has two ivory tusks, one of which grows long and curved and handsome. He is called a narwhal, and although fewer men have tasted him than have tasted either whale or elephant, his skin is reported to be delicious, crisp as celery and tasting of nuts and mushroom – and looking like half-inch thick linoleum, which for me at least would prove an esthetic handicap.'

(M. F. K. Fisher)

There are plenty of travellers' and cooks' accounts in this book that include recommendations as to fitting provisions for a particular occasion or journey; that important business is the prelude to most accounts of travelling food and picnics. In Hong Kong forgetting the ice or the lemons, the unfailing necessities of boating picnics, may have been grounds for divorce but not a matter of life and death. For expeditions to extreme destinations like Everest and Antarctica, mistakes or omissions in provisioning could tip the balance, already slight enough, between success or failure and the loss of life against which gung ho fortitude, tweed plus fours and a good dose of British phlegm was hollow insurance. The deaths of all members of Sir John Franklin's famously failed expedition to find the North West Passage in 1845 has been in part at least attributed to contaminated tinned foods in the earliest days of the tinning process, trichinosis from infested polar bear meat and straightforward starvation that may or may not have resulted in cases of cannibalism. The provisions, perishables and preserves of picnic and travel food and the requirements for cooking and eating it are worth close attention.

The apparently amateur nature of Captain Scott's 1901-1904 'Discovery Expedition' to Antarctica did not preclude considerable research into suitable rations that included advice from Fridtjof Nansen, the Norwegian Arctic explorer. We are now aware that Scott was a good deal more professional in his preparations than suited the idea of the British hero at the time. In a letter to Sir Clements Markham, President of the Royal Geographic Society and major supporter of the National Antarctic Expedition, Nansen recommends the Stavanger Preserving Company, now a museum, as providers of 'tinned mackerel', 'excellent, the very best food we had aboard' and *fiskefarce*, 'something we never got tired of eating'.

This recipe comes from *For Danish Appetites:*

Fiskefars (Fish forcemeat)

1lb lean white fish; 4 tablespoons potato; 3 tablespoons melted butter;
2 tbsp each flour and cornflour; 1 teaspoon salt; pepper;
1 egg well beaten; 1/2c. Milk

Grind fish, using the fine blade on your grinder, or whirl in a blender, a little at a time, until all is smooth. Add butter, flour and cornstarch. Add seasoning to taste, and beaten egg. Mix very well, using an electric mixer. Gradually add milk, beating constantly, until absorbed. This mixture can either be fried in spoonfuls or baked as fiskebudding : butter a 1 quart mould and sprinkle with breadcrumbs. Add the fiskefars. Set mould in a pan of hot water and bake in oven 325° for 1 hour.

This makes 4 servings.

Scott himself was closely involved with the proper provisioning of the expedition, following up an order for 1,000 pounds of Cartridge Pemmican to the American Compressed Food Co. in Passaic, New Jersey on 23rd April, 1901, with another letter on 25th asking for only 500lbs to be delivered since:

> It has been pointed out that your pemmican contains 43% only of Ox Lard. This is not serious, but compared with other pemmicans, the nutritive value is, I regret to say, not satisfactory.

In fact, as Nansen may well have pointed out, the expedition diet would have been improved and more likely to stave off the scurvy suffered by its members with less preserved and more of the fresh meat available from seals, penguins, and, as they turned out to be of little use to the British with no idea how to use them in their sledges, their dogs. Supplies, including black and white pepper and mustard, rum, butter, lime juice, tea and chocolate foods, were inspected by the Government Laboratory. This may have been a sensible precaution given reports showing that one pemmican sample 'contained pieces of steel, probably from the machinery with which prepared, weighing rather more than half an ounce'. The testing of all tins was essential for the importance of them being 'free from taint'.

The laboratory report finds 'somatose' unsuitable, 'said to be processed from beef but is tasteless and contains no characteristic substance it is impossible to trace its precise origin.' The description of somatose in *The Wide Encyclopedia of Cookery. An Encyclopedic Handbook for the Homemaker covering Foods and Beverages-their Purchase, Preparation, and Service* adds further detail: 'Beef Somatose is a commercial product used in invalid diets, somatose is a granular predigested meat powder which contains a large amount of albumin and is free of peptones. It has a yellowish color and a faint taste and odor. Dissolved in water it forms a light yellow solution having almost no taste or odor.' Nutritious or not, it sounds too horrible for words.

The 'Food list for three years with quantities and costs for 40 men' included:

3,000 lbs roast beef
750 lbs roast kidney
750 lbs rabbit
250 lbs tripe and onions
16,000 Cabin biscuits
25,000 Extra Navy (biscuits)

'Medical comforts' of:
25 gallons each of brandy and whisky
36 gallons of sherry
25 gallons of virol
75 gallons of Devonshire cream
150 gallons each of chicken and mutton broth
576 of Nestlés and Viking milk

Assorted sauces, including wild cherry, perhaps to accompany the tinned duck; 200lbs of egg powder, 800 gallons of rum to be dispensed 2 ounces daily per man (the standard Navy ration from 1850-1970), 1,800lbs tobacco (1lb monthly), 3,500lbs cheddar.

On the 7th May 1900, Clements Markham's *Report to Hygiene Committee* points out that 'preserved potatoes are not good but it is said that if frozen potatoes are plunged at once into boiling water without previous thawing, they are found to be perfectly good as regards taste. This deserves consideration'

He also suggests the carrying of livestock in large enough quantities to be killed and frozen 'as soon as the temperature is low enough, to which might perhaps be added seal and penguin flesh sufficient to last through a winter'.

The invoice from 'Maconochie Bros. Ltd, Manufacturers of jams, pickles, sauces, soups, preserved fish & meats of all kinds' of July 6th 1901 comes to £1,437.. 5 shillings and 7 pence.

Harrods Stores Ltd were the suppliers for the British National Antarctic Expedition relief ship *Morning*, providing, with barrels of salt beef; the Plasmon (homogenised) beef; tins of jugged hare and partridges; a large supply of tinned vegetables; preserved and dried fruits; various tinned fish, halibut, salmon, gurnet, soles; pickles and chutneys and 200 ¼ lb tins of curry powder plus other spices. It sounds just what you would expect in an old fashioned country house larder but on a larger scale. I remember tinned ham and others which never could live up to the labels on the tin however grand their retailer. It must be said that by and large tins originating in France, whether of foie gras, coq au vin or petit pois, more usually exceeded anticipation. Good or bad, all those tins sat higgledy piggledy on mid-20th century larder shelves awaiting the nuclear winter and rusting gently until their lids popped, a clearer indication of inedibility than any sell by date.

Harrods also provided the wherewithal for serving all this food; sauce tureens and ladles; egg cups and a desert set; fish carvers and toast racks; napkins, oven cloths and fancy dinner mats; cut table bottles and 24 champagne glasses.   With the tents, mats and other necessities, there is an order for one dog basket.

Everest Expeditions.

The receipt for goods to be sent to the 'Mount Everest Expedition, Darjeeling via Calcutta' on the 27th January 1922 listed '30 tins of Heinz Spaghetti' and 120 of Harris sausages from the old factory in Calne, Wiltshire; 60 tins of quail in foie gras (travellers in the 1920s got through a lot of foie gras wherever in the world they were); HP, Harvey's and Lea & Perrins Worcestershire sauces; acid and pear drops; 80 jars of Bovril; 30 tins of grape nuts, the cure all cereal invented at the end of the 19th century; and 30 2lb plum puddings, the essential traveller's treat so recommended by Colonel Kenney Herbert and Elizabeth David and, as part of a successful diet for soldiers, by Alexis Soyer. With freight charges, the Army & Navy's invoice came to £873 eight shillings and eleven pence.

For the famous 1924 expedition, during which Mallory may or may not have reached the summit of the mountain, Fortnum & Mason provided four sets of condiments, salt, pepper and mustard; vegetable dishes with covers; sauce boats; and 3½ dozen soup plates, presumably anticipating a high rate of attrition. In a note on the food Mallory wrote: 'It is impossible to please all tastes, and a working compromise must be made'; on marmalade: 'everybody likes Coopers'. There was an important question to answer over another important requirement, the champagne, 'what brand?' ten blocks of parkin, a North of England ginger cake with oatmeal and treacle, from Shaws of Kendal but none of the famous Kendal mint cake, probably invented in the mid-19th century and eaten on the summit of Everest by Hillary and Tensing in 1953. Jam was to be supplied in tins. 'These should be made with thin tops which can be readily cut with the ordinary pen knife'. (*Records from Royal Geographical Society Archives*)

The first successful ascent of Annapurna by a French team in 1950 nearly ended in complete disaster when the monsoon broke on the descent. Maurice Herzog, leader of the team, lost fingers and toes from frostbite and other members of the party suffered associated injuries. On the expedition's reunion at the lowest camp, the celebratory nature of the event, their survival as much as their conquest of the mountain, warranted the opening and sharing of their one bottle of champagne and the 'one and only tin of chicken in aspic'. (Maurice Herzog, *Annapurna*)

Provisions, whether comestibles or the utensils for cooking and eating, have been pared down considerably since the days of the earliest explorations and expeditions although books on high altitude trekking and climbing still contain long lists of necessities. The covered vegetable dishes are long gone in favour of plastic cups, a knife, fork and spoon, a plate, bowl and plastic water bottles with the odd pot for cooking and a gas or paraffin camping stove. As for the food, sherpa porridge and chapattis have taken over from partridges and plum puddings.

Ranulph Fiennes book of his 1992/1993 Antarctic crossing with Dr Mike Stroud, *Mind Over Matter*, has a photograph of a member of Captain Scott's expedition sitting on a box of Heinz baked bean tins, a sponsorship obligation equally required by the makers of dehydrated foods carried by today's polar travellers. With their greater understanding of the body's requirements for survival under the most extreme conditions, contemporary explorers nonetheless still suffer greatly for their triumphs. To carry enough calories to sustain life, however freeze-dried and lightweight they may be, remains a besetting problem and becomes an almost all-consuming focus for the intrepid explorer.

> 'Food took the place of sex, anticipated with salivating eagerness and savoured to the last lick. In three days' time we must switch to cut rations, to prolong the number of travel days left to us, by making up for the six rations we had cannibalised to date.
>
> Now that the physical struggle of the 800-mile, 11,000-foot ascent was behind us our calorie expenditure had dropped from an appalling 10,000 to about 7,000 per day. Our standard ration of 5,200 calories per day would shortly be cut to 3,000, which is the amount a healthy male teenager expects to consume in everyday life conditions.
>
> Our current sorry state had largely been caused by the long weeks of calorie deficiency. As Mike put it, "Our calorie deficit

has been the equivalent of the total input of a normal person. It is exactly as though a normal person had eaten nothing, I repeat nothing, all this time. After several weeks they would get weak and desperately hungry. In fact they would starve. We are slowly starving".

This, of course, was a godsend for Mike's research work. After sixty days of watching Mike divide our daily ration in two and hand me one vitamin tablet, four small-size milk chocolate bars, eight sheets of loo paper (inedible) and one crunchy flapjack, I began to nurse horrible suspicions that he was handing me the smaller of the flapjacks every day. This irked me as I grew more ravenous until, on the sixty-first day, I suggested that we take turns to choose the daily flapjacks. Mike agreed readily enough.'

When Jeffa Murray, the first female helicopter pilot to fly solo round the world, followed up in 2003 by an attempt to fly from pole to pole, she was also going to meet her husband, Simon, in Antarctica on his quest to become the oldest man to walk to the South Pole beside the explorer Pen Hadow. Weight implications required both husband and wife to survive largely on dehydrated food but communication afforded by satellite phone allowed Simon to order up more solid supplies for helicopter delivery to the Pole – bacon, eggs, butter and a frying pan.

Isabella Bird, the Victorian traveller who, except when travelling, suffered ill health all her life, especially during her mid-life six years marriage to Edinburgh doctor John Bishop, had a great deal to say on all aspects of the countries she visited. The 'Food Question' for her travels in Japan gets its fair share of acerbic comment and she deals with it entirely to her own satisfaction. One gets the feeling from her letters to her sister that her diet during her tour may indeed have consisted largely of tea and rice enlivened presumably with her meagre personal supplies and the occasional 'fowl of much experience'.

'If I accepted much of the advice given to me, as to taking tinned meats and soups, claret, and a Japanese maid, I should need a train of at least six pack-horses. 'The "Food Question" is said to be the most important one for all travellers, and it is discussed continually with startling earnestness, not alone as regards my tour. However apathetic people are on other subjects, the mere mention of this one rouses them into interest. All have suffered or may suffer, and every one wishes to impart his own experience or to learn from that of others. Foreign ministers, professors, missionaries, merchants - all discuss it with becoming gravity as a question of life and death, which by many it is supposed to be. The fact is that, except at a few hotels in popular resorts which are got up for foreigners, bread, butter, milk, meat, poultry, coffee, wine, and beer, are unattainable, that fresh fish is rare, and that unless one can live on rice, tea, and eggs, with the addition now and then of some tasteless fresh vegetables, food must be taken, as the fishy and vegetable abominations known as "Japanese food" can only be swallowed and digested by a few, and that after long practice.

'The "Food Question" has been solved by a modified rejection of all advice! I have only brought a small supply of Liebig's extract of meat, 4 lbs. of raisins, some chocolate, both for eating and drinking, and some brandy in case of need. 'When we stopped at wayside tea-houses the runners bathed their feet, rinsed their mouths, and ate rice, pickles, salt fish, and "broth of abominable things", after which they smoked their tiny pipes, which give them three whiffs for each filling. As soon as I got out at any of these, one smiling girl brought me the tabako-bon, a square wood or lacquer tray, with a china or bamboo charcoal-holder and ash-pot upon it, and another presented me with a zen, a small lacquer table about six inches high, with a tiny teapot with a hollow handle at right angles with the spout, holding about an English tea-cupful, and two cups without handles or saucers, with a capacity of from ten to twenty thimblefuls each. The hot water is merely allowed to rest a minute on the tea-leaves, and the infusion is a clear straw-coloured liquid with a delicious aroma and flavour, grateful and refreshing at all times. If Japanese tea "stands," it acquires a coarse bitterness and an unwholesome astringency. Milk and sugar are not used. A clean-looking wooden or lacquer pail with a lid is kept in all tea-houses, and though hot rice, except to order, is only ready three times daily, the pail always contains cold rice, and the coolies heat it by pouring hot tea over it. As you eat, a tea-house girl, with this pail beside her, squats on the floor in front of you, and fills your rice bowl till you say, "Hold, enough!" On this road it is expected that you leave three or four sen on the tea-tray for a rest of an hour or two and tea.' (*Unbeaten Tracks in Japan, An Account of Travels in the Interior including Visits to the Aborigines of Yezo and the Shrine of Nikko*)

The 'food question' arises again in more comic form in *Three Men in a Boat*, the matter of travelling with cheese being particularly vexatious.

'For other breakfast things, George suggested eggs and bacon, which were easy to cook, cold meat, tea, bread and butter, and jam. For lunch, he said, we could have biscuits, cold meat, bread and butter, and jam - but NO CHEESE. Cheese, like oil, makes too much of itself. It wants the whole boat to itself. It goes through the hamper, and gives a cheesy flavour to everything else there. You can't tell whether you are eating apple-pie or German sausage, or strawberries and cream. It all seems cheese. There is too much odour about cheese.

I remember a friend of mine, buying a couple of cheeses at Liverpool. Splendid cheeses they were, ripe and mellow, and with a two hundred horse-power scent about them that might have been warranted to carry three miles, and knock a man over at two hundred yards.

Fond as I am of cheese, therefore, I hold that George was right in declining to take any.

"We shan't want any tea," said George (Harris's face fell at this); "but we'll have a good round, square, slap-up meal at seven - dinner, tea, and supper combined."

Harris grew more cheerful. George suggested meat and fruit pies, cold meat, tomatoes, fruit, and green stuff. For drink, we took some wonderful sticky concoction of Harris's, which you mixed with water and called lemonade, plenty of tea, and a bottle of whisky, in case, as George said, we got upset.

(Jerome K Jerome *Three Men in a Boat*)

Fynes Morrison's *Itinerary* gives a clear picture of the travel food of the late 16th century, which, in the Mediterranean at least, doesn't sound too bad at all, especially given the liberal quantities of wine he lists. For our enjoyment he also gives brief sketches of some of his fellow travellers and consumers.

'This Fleming was a fat man, borne to consume victuals, & he had now spent in his journey to Venice thirty pound sterling, and here for his journey to Jerusalem had already put into the ship full Hogs-heads of Wine, and store of all victuals, when suddenly he changed his minde, for feare of a great Rhume wherewith he was troubled, or being discouraged with the difficulty of the journey, and would needs returne to Emden, with purpose (if hee were to be believed) to returne the next Spring to some place neere Jerusalem, in an English ship, which he thought more commodious. He professed, that he had put much money out upon his returne, and since hee was old, and very sickly, and after so long a journey, and so much money spent, would needes returne home, I cannot thinke that he ever undertooke this journey againe.'

The *Itinerary* describes in careful detail the fresh food supplied by his ship's Master for the first few days out of port en route from Cyprus to Joppa (Jaffa), that was followed by hard 'bisket', salt or pickled fish for fasting days, 'oyle in stead of butter, nuts, fruit, cheese and like things'. Fynes and his brother took emergency rations of their own of dried fruit, 'very white bisket' and naturally 'some flaggons of rich wine', not neglecting ginger and nutmeg 'to comfort our stomackes in case of weakness' and other remedies for chills and agues 'some cooling sirops, and some pounds of sugar, and some laxative medicines'. Such precautions were well taken in the face of a barrel of wine that 'fretted our very intrals' for a cost of 'one Zechine, and foure soldi of Venice, and two Turkish aspers'.

A century and a half or so later, the novelist Tobias Smollett, wrote his *Travels through France and Italy*. His views on the importance of carrying his own food and supplies in order to avoid the expense and dubious quality of the food available at the wayside auberge are a foretaste of those later opinions of Mrs Jekyll and Sir Francis Colchester Wemyss in the first half of the 20th century. Smollet was a curious enough traveller but one has a sense that he was the sort who would rather have observed what foreigners ate than eat it himself; he invariably sounds surprised when he finds something that he likes. In another era he would definitely have carried his own cornflakes on trips abroad, and a pot of Marmite.

> 'For my part, I hate the French cookery, and abominate garlic, with which all their ragouts in this part of the country are highly seasoned: we therefore formed a different plan of living upon the road. Before we left Paris, we laid in a stock of tea, chocolate, cured neats' tongues, and saucissons, or Bologna sausages, both of which we found in great perfection in that capital, where, indeed, there are excellent provisions of all sorts. About ten in the morning we stopped to breakfast at some auberge, where we always found bread, butter, and milk. In the mean time, we ordered a poulard or two to be roasted, and these, wrapped in a napkin, were put into the boot of the coach, together with bread, wine, and water. About two or three in the afternoon, while the horses were changing, we laid a cloth upon our knees, and producing our store, with a few earthen plates,discussed our short meal without further ceremony. This was followed by a dessert of grapes and other fruit, which we had also provided. I must own I found these transient refreshments much more agreeable than any regular meal I ate upon the road.'

It sounds perfectly delicious, especially those freshly roasted poulards, however scrawny they may have been, kept just short of cold in their napkin. Nevertheless by the time of his return to England, Smollet is rather depressingly forswearing alcohol including the picnic wine.

'For they may boast of their wine as they please; but that which is drank by the common people, not only here, but also in all the wine countries of France, is neither so strong, nourishing, nor (in my opinion) so pleasant to the taste as the small-beer of England. It must be owned that all the peasants who have wine for their ordinary drink are of a diminutive size, in comparison of those who use milk, beer, or even water; and it is a constant observation, that when there is a scarcity of wine, the common people are always more healthy, than in those seasons when it abounds. The longer I live, the more I am convinced that wine, and all fermented liquors, are pernicious to the human constitution; and that for the preservation of health, and exhilaration of the spirits, there is no beverage comparable to simple water.'

Plenty of other travellers have taken their drinking water seriously, most fear the ill-effects of a contaminated supply. For Hindus travelling out of India in the days before Indians became so well and widely travelled, the journey across the 'Black Water' involved worse possibilities than loss of a current life. Questions of caste and religious purity were of particular importance in the case of rulers whose position could easily be undermined by any perceived loss of status. Maharajah Madho Singh of Jaipur, summonsed to England for the coronation of the King Emperor, Edward VII, in 1901, commissioned two gigantic silver vessels, to carry the holy Ganges water for his personal consumption if he was to avoid religious pollution. They are now in the City Palace in Jaipur, each has a capacity of 9000 litres.

In the Colonies as in Europe, travellers, whether bent on the pleasures of the picnic or forced by work or circumstance onto the roads and a life on the move, were advised, as we have seen in other chapters, at the least to carry their most essential and basic provisions. This did not as a rule involve carrying water great distances but enough only to survive from one water hole, stream, well or oasis to the next. Today's tourists and campers have fits at the thought of local water and cannot survive a couple of hours in even temperate climates without their rucksacks and multi-pocketed waistcoats bristling with plastic bottled water; they would no more trust water of unlabelled or local provenance for their hydration than would the Maharajah.

For the explorer in unknown territory, the problem was not so much what water as where there might next be water. On his journey across the Empty Quarter, Wilfrid Thesiger's fear of running out of water and food for both men and camels was constant.

> Our water was nearly finished and there was only enough flour for about another week. The starving camels were so thirsty that they had refused to eat some half-dried herbage which we had passed. We must water them in the next day or two or they would collapse. Al-Auf said that it would take us three more days to reach Khaba well in Dhafara, but that there was a very brackish well not far away. He thought the camels might drink its water.
>
> Next day, after seven hours' travelling, we reached Khaur Sabakha on the edge of the Dhafara sands. We cleaned out the well and found brackish water at seven feet, so bitter that even the camels only drank a little before refusing it. They sniffed thirstily at the water with which al Auf tried to coax them from a leather bucket, but only dipped their lips into it. We covered their noses but still they would not drink. Yet al Auf said that

Arabs themselves drank this water mixed with milk, and when I expressed my disbelief he added that if an Arab was really thirsty he would even kill a camel and drink the liquid in its stomach, or ram a stick down its throat and drink the vomit. We went on again till nearly sunset.

Next day we remained where we were. Hamad said that he would go for news and return the following day. Al Auf, who went with him, came back in the afternoon with two skins full of water which, although slightly brackish, was delicious after the filthy evil-smelling dregs we had drunk the night before.

For years the Empty Quarter had represented to me the final, unattainable challenge which the desert offered. Suddenly it had come within my reach. I remembered my excitement when Lean had casually offered me the chance to go there, the immediate determination to cross it, and then the doubts and fears, the frustrations, and the moments of despair. Now I had crossed it. To others my journey would have little importance. It would produce nothing except a rather inaccurate map which no one was ever likely to use. It was a personal experience, and the reward had been a drink of clean, nearly tasteless water. I was content with that.   (*Arabian Sands*)

In India, on the matter of more solid refreshments, Colonel Kenney Herbert is, as always, ready to advise on suitable provisions for 'the office snacklet, the lunch in the train, or al fresco out shooting'. For a 'lunch-let' he suggests a roll with cheese and plantains but 'the taste of eating cheese with fruit is, I fear, un-English'. For the traveller the 'digester pot', elsewhere in Anglo-Indian books described as the 'pepper-pot' was an essential addition to travelling supplies; 'filled with stewed steak and oysters, or some equally toothsome stew'.

The *Anglo-Indian's Vade Mecum* gives clear instructions as to the contents of the pepper-pot:

The evening before starting on a journey, put in a fowl, one or two pounds of mutton chops, some potatoes and onions – in fact any meat and any vegetables, a due proportion of water, salt, pepper, and spices, and then allow all to boil slowly, or stew, for as long as is necessary. Now add a little Worcestershire sauce or Harvey sauce, for piquancy, and the whole is ready. Take the pot with you, and on arriving at the halting station, heat it up again, and set it on the table.

The trick was then to refill the pot with more chops or any available game like jungle fowl, vegetables and, for good measure, a few hard-boiled eggs; boiling and refilling nightly for the rest of the journey which presents a rather horrible picture of the contents and notwithstanding the fact that: 'Some travellers look upon the pepper-pot as sacred, and never allow their servants even to look into it, the lid being kept padlocked. This is not a bad plan if your servants are low fellows, and not to be trusted, otherwise it is demoralising, and hurts their feelings, without affording any adequate compensation.' (*The European in India or Anglo-Indian's Vade Mecum*)

David Burton in *The Raj at Table* says these stew ups were better known as 'all blaze' and survived on trips up country into the 1930s. The mixture was improved by a foundation of 'tickle gummy', a combination of game stock and claret. The thought of that endlessly boiled pot in which the bottom is never quite reached, makes one sympathise with Colonel Kenney Herbert's belief that in reality, 'A cold lunch is the best for the open air'.

'A home-made brawn of tongue, a part of an ox head, and sheep's trotters, well seasoned, and slightly spiced, was another *spécialité*. 'A nice piece of the brisket of beef salted and spiced, boiled, placed under a weight, and then trimmed into a neat shape (the trimmings come in for sandwiches, potted-meat, or "bubble and squeak") is a very handy thing for the tiffin basket; and a much respected patron of mine recommends for travelling, a really good cold plum pudding in which a glass of brandy has been included. Cake is acceptable at every kind of luncheon; in fact, cakes were invented for that meal, for 5 o'clock tea, weddings, and for school-boys only.'

The picnic as an entertainment in Anglo-Indian circles was not expected to be a simple affair. In 1904, Constance E. Gordon, while strongly advocating the excellence of 'savoury sandwiches' at teatime, does not, according to her list for a picnic for twelve, consider them suitable food for an alfresco entertainment where the butler is required to 'make a nice French Salad to go round with the Cold Meats'. Her menu is well thought out and perhaps not of excessive quantity for the time although 6lbs of cold beef besides ham, turkey, ox-tongue, pigeon pie and soused pomfrets would certainly be heavy on the protein for contemporary taste.

(Constance Eveline Gordon, *The Anglo-Indian Cuisine*)

Royal and Imperial

'The six royal hampers packed for such occasions contained such items as cold clear soup, lobster mayonnaise, cold trout, plovers' eggs, cold duck, chicken, lamb cutlets, ham and tongue, a selection of sandwiches, a choice of some four desserts and Parisian pastries. Gold plate was taken along as well to remind the King that it was a royal meal, even if it came from hampers.'

(Edward VII's opera picnic described in *Dinner at Buckingham Palace*)

Queen Victoria's accounts of her rustic Scottish picnics suggest her enjoyment of more impromptu events; the current Queen is also a veteran of Scottish picnics at Balmoral as well as barbecues on isolated beaches when sailing round the Western Isles on summer tours; she will undoubtedly have been equally plagued by the worst of Scottish pests.

'One of the Duke's keepers had prepared a fire and got a kettle boiling, and where we took our tea. Afterwards sketched, but we were surrounded by a perfect cloud of midges which bit me terribly.'

Victoria's Highland Journals are full of outings, picnic lunches and teas that sound very unlike our picture of the formal and mournful stuffiness of her court elsewhere.

'At half past two we five ladies lunched upon a heathery knoll, just above Mr Keir's wood, and were indeed glad to do so, as

we were tired by the great heat. As soon as luncheon was over, we walked down through the woods, a few hundred yards to where the carriage was. Here we took leave, with much regret, of the dear kind Duchess and amiable Miss McGregor. The evening was quite splendid, the sky yellow and pink and the distant hills coming out soft and blue, both behind, and in front of us. At a place called Loch-na-braig - we stopped, and while Grant ran back to get from a small house some hot water in the kettle, we three, with Brown's help, scrambled over a low stone wall by the roadside, and lit a fire and prepared our tea.'
(Queen Victoria, *More Leaves from a Highland Journal*)

Coronations are interminable and exhausting events for all those involved. After the coronation of George V, several peers admitted to the *Illustrated London News* their concern that the butter in the greaseproof wrapped sandwiches concealed in the linings of their coronets might have begun to melt and leak (Juliet Nicholson, *The Perfect Summer*). Queen Victoria wrote of repairing to St Edward's Chapel after her coronation in Westminster Abbey which Lord Melbourne described as more unlike a chapel than anywhere he had ever seen with the altar covered in sandwiches and bottles of wine (*Queen Victoria's Letters*, 28th June 1838).

Before Queen Elizabeth II's coronation in 1953, the American audience were fascinated by the idea of peers hiding sandwiches in their coronets and were enlightened further by Mrs Doris Langley-Moore, director of London's Museum of Costume, lecturing round the USA and answering questions about the ceremony.

'This is not an eccentricity. In fact most coronets are fitted with ribbons inside to keep the sandwiches in place. For most of the ceremony they rest in the laps of the nobles. As they have to sit patiently from seven in the morning until late in the afternoon, we can hardly blame them from nibbling sandwiches from their jewelled lunch pails. I am told that some of the peers bring other sustenance besides sandwiches.'
(*Rome News-Tribune*, May 20th 1953)

I have a friend, an artist, whose usually avant garde instincts do not preclude an insistence that no picnic is complete without coronation chicken. I admit, however clichéd it has become, to sharing a weakness for cool creamy curry sauce mixed with carefully skinned, boned, poached chicken, albeit not actually a dish invented for outdoor eating. Constance Spry wrote that for the 300 people at the Coronation lunch, the curry was barely detectable and almost certainly unrecognised by the diners, adding 'mainly, a delicate and nut-like flavour' to the finished dish. That mysterious hint of curry might have been the inspiration for the rather horrible 1970s dinner party favourite, Snaffles mousse, invented at the eponymous restaurant in Dublin. A mixture of tinned consommé, Philadelphia cream cheese and curry powder that supposedly made this beige concoction taste of smoked fish, as if that would have necessarily been an advantage. The brief amusement was in forcing uninitiated guests to guess the ingredients but there was little pleasure in eating the stuff however gaily garnished with prawns and obscuring greenery.

We have moved on a long way since 1953 and even since 1971. 'Curry' of one sort or another has become a British national dish and Rosemary Hume's original recipe, a dessert spoon of curry powder for sauce to mix with ¾ pint of mayonnaise plus the odd tablespoon or so of whipped cream, is a little light on the spice for most contemporary tastes. As to the mayonnaise, Elizabeth David said pretty much all there is to be said about bottles and jars of the stuff in her article, *The True Emulsion*. We have been educated far beyond vilified salad cream since her article was published in the *Spectator* in 1962 and most of us are very well accustomed to the taste of good olive oil. In fact the best olive oil from the plethora of available choices is far too olivey on its own and makes a bitter mayonnaise unless diluted with something lighter. As for an oil to disappear into all that curry and cream – groundnut will do beautifully and can be used as well to fry the onions for the curry sauce.

Coronation Chicken

Coronation chicken is usually served with cold rice or a rice salad, the simpler the better, with only chopped peeled tomatoes and a handful of chopped or torn herbs mixed into the rice while still hot, a little olive oil, lemon juice, plenty of ground black pepper and a pinch of sea salt crumbled in the fingers. Cold but not chilled new potatoes are equally good and feel less stodgy with the creamy sauce, while toasted pine nuts or shredded almonds add extra crunch to the chicken.

George V's Balmoral picnics, remembered from her childhood by Loelia, Duchess of Westminster, whose father was Head of the Royal Household, sound carefully planned, well-staffed, but fairly relaxed occasions. Somehow one can imagine the rather homely little figure of Queen Victoria sitting in the heather but stately Queen Mary without a chair is unthinkable.

'One of the yearly jollifications was the Royal Picnic. A large party met on the shores of Loch Muick near a small lodge called the Glassalt which was more or less untouched since the days of Queen Victoria. The lake was full of brown trout and a ghillie used to row some way from the shore with a long net which he paid out as he went along; then this was slowly dragged in, the younger members of the party dashing into the water to help haul it in. We gathered up the silver slithering fish in buckets and took them to the chef who, in full regalia, white cap and all, was ready with a hot fire. The King and Queen sat on chairs and the rest of us sprawled in the heather and the royal footmen (in mufti) brought us the fish fry which was as delicious as anything that I have ever tasted.'

A biography of George V further describes the 'well-regulated luxury' of those picnics when 'a cortège of huge maroon Daimlers with gold-plated radiators lurched along bumpy tracks to disgorge baskets of food and guests in tweed shooting suits, hats and well polished brogues. Women, similarly clad in respect of suitable Scottish tweed, were not encouraged to wear trousers even when riding, which presents an improbable picture of an elegant rider in long riding skirt sitting side saddle on a small hairy highland pony.

The King's taste for good food and a level of luxury was by no means inevitable in royalty. Perhaps it may partially be accounted for by memories of five teenage years spent as a midshipman, firstly on board the training ship *Britannia*, in Devon.

> 'It never did me any good to be a Prince, I can tell you, and many was the time I wished I hadn't been. Then we had a sort of tuck- shop on land, up the steep hill; only we weren't allowed to bring eatables into the ship, and they used to search you as you came aboard. Well, the big boys used to fag me to bring them back a whole lot of stuff – and I was always found out and got into trouble in addition to having the stuff confiscated. And the worst of it was, it was always my money; they never paid me back –'
> (Kenneth Rose, *King George V* - to Sir Owen Morshead)

Three years on HMS *Bacchante* in the 1880s encouraged enjoyment of better things during occasional visits to exotic ports; shellfish, turtle, pineapples and avocado pears no doubt made regular ship's fare even more disagreeable. 'Weeks and weeks at sea, sometimes very monotonous weeks, living on food that was more than monotonous, and also exceedingly nasty. Mostly salt pork and ship's biscuit. Remember, there were no comforts in those days. No such thing as electrical freezing plant. So fresh vegetables, fruit and fresh provisions lasted a very, very short time after leaving harbour.' (Cdr. G.W Hillyard, *Ideal Shipmate*)

The Queen's picnics in the days of summer cruises on her Royal Yacht, *Britannia*, were organised with naval precision, clear responsibilities apportioned to the various crew departments on board. 'When Members of the Royal Family go on a picnic the Boatswain is responsible for co-ordinating the arrangements for landing, and for preparation of the equipment on shore.'

Royal Barge Crew - Tents (2)
Tent pole, feet, guys and pegs
Ground sheets
Shovel

Royal Apartments - Food and drink hampers
Blankets
Games (buckets, spades, balls)
Skis, fins, etc

Engine Room - Barbeques (2) and associated utensils
Fuel
Gas Lamps (2)
DC Lamps (if required)
(Note: In addition 1 MEM is to accompany the barbeques as the stoker).

Communications - Portable Radio (ICOM)
Radio Operator (if required)'

(List from Royal Yacht *Britannia*)

In 1939, the Queen's parents, George VI and Queen Elizabeth visited Canada and the USA on a mission to build support for Great Britain at a time of increasing fears of war in Europe. 'After two days in Washington, the tone of the royal couple's visit transformed from formal to informal as they accompanied the Roosevelts to their home in Hyde Park, New York. The King and Queen's stay in Hyde Park illustrated to the American people that although they were royalty, they also enjoyed the simpler things in life. FDR brought the couple to his new hilltop retreat - Top Cottage - on the eastern portion of his estate for an old-fashioned, American-style picnic. Much to the horror of FDR's mother Sara Roosevelt, the King and Queen of England were served hot dogs on the front porch of the cottage.

Although the press made a great deal of the hotdogs (the picnic made the front page of the *New York Times*), the menu also included slightly more delicate fare considered fit for a King and Queen:'

In fact, just as Queen Victoria enjoyed her simple Scottish teas, there is every chance that such a simple and relaxed lunch would have appealed no end to the King and Queen. Queen Elizabeth's younger daughter, Princess Margaret, was considered demanding, autocratic and much on her royal dignity – one imagines with regal tastes to match. Notes in her hand on her chef's menu book offer an alternative view of an interested and courteous woman in close contact with her staff and the planning of straightforward and distinctly picnicky dinners for small groups of friends after the ballet or theatre; a 'picnic with steaks' or 'a cold chicken with lovely salads' that could be taken and eaten at the theatre. (Leo Groden, *My Royal Cookbook*)

FDR's elder brother James, otherwise known as Rosy, had an encounter, during childhood travels in Europe with his family, with the immediate descendants of a more parvenu royal, the Emperor Napoleon I of France.

> Rosy made friends with three French children who were staying at the hotel with their parents, the Count and Countess Alexandre Walewski. The Count was the president of the French Legislative Assembly and the natural child of Napoleon I and Marie Walewska of Poland. One morning the Roosevelts and Walewskis rode out into the countryside to a wooded park where the children played beneath the great trees while their parents sat on blankets and ate their lunch of cherries and milk. They returned to the hotel just in time for dinner, Rebecca remembered, 'loaded with wild-flowers and roses, the children in a gale'.
>
> (Geoffrey Ward, *Before the Trumpet: Young Franklin Roosevelt, 1882-1905*)

Marcel Boulestin's Clafoutis (Cherry Cake Limousin)

'The clafoutis is a kind of flan or cake made with batter and cherries and special to the Limousin. The best cherries for this purpose are the soft black ones with a rather acid taste. For the batter take six ounces of flour, make a hole in the middle, put in a little salt and, one by one three eggs well beaten, then water; mix well and add more water till the batter is the right consistency (it should be a little thicker than batter for pancakes). Flavour with a puddingspoonful of either rum, brandy or kirsch. Then add half a pound of cherries and pour the mixture in a well-buttered mould. Cook for about three-quarters of an hour to one hour in a fairly hot oven. When the clafoutis is cooked turn it out of the mould and sprinkle with a great deal of sugar. It is usually eaten tepid or cold. The mould should be a rather shallow one, like those used for open tarts. In Limousin the cherries are not stoned and no sugar is put in the batter.'

(X Marcel Boulestin, *Recipes of Boulestin*)

A royal picnic in India was a less simple pleasure and one with which George V would have been comfortable. Elizabeth David quotes Charles Baskerville, the long-lived American portrait painter, whose images of India include drawings of royal hunting cheetahs and pet tigers, describing a picnic given by the Maharajah in Jaipur in 1937.

> 'Yesterday we spent the whole day picnicking... a lorry with lunch and bottles followed our car....one thing I particularly like about these outdoor luncheons is the cold fried fish. Besides the European food there are always some spicy Indian dishes... cold curry of boar's head (without the eyes) or peppery leaves of spinach fried in batter... of course a hamper of whisky, beer, gimlets, cider, and water is always taken along.'

> (*South Wind Through the Kitchen, The Best of Elizabeth David*)

Jennifer Brennan describes the Maharaja of Orcha's catering arrangements during a two day tiger shoot.

> 'The guests sat at round table and were served with thalis with the food arranged in silver bowls. There were chicken and meat curries, birds and game, lentil dishes and hot chapattis and parathas passed around by the servants. Boiled rice was in the middle of every tray. After the meal, silver bowls of scented water were passed around for the guests to wash their hands.' (*Curries and Bugles*)

In her book *Royal Indian Cookery*, Manju Shivraj Singh, the niece of the last Maharani of Jaipur, disappointingly omits a recipe for boar's head curry, with or without the eyes, but these venison kebabs, *Hiran ke kebab*, would make a robust picnic dish.

Venison Kebabs

I kg of boneless venison, 425 ml water, 2 onions, 6 cloves garlic, 30ml roasted poppy seeds, 12 blanched almonds, 2 whole dried red chillis, 5ml cumin seeds, salt to taste, 100g chickpea flour, 125ml oil for frying.

Filling: 2 onions, 2 green chillis, 2.5cm piece fresh root ginger, small bunch fresh coriander of mint, chopped.

Cut the venison into bite-sized cubes and bring to boil in heavy based saucepan with water, lower heat and simmer until all moisture has evaporated. Mince the meat in a food processor and put on one side.

Mince onions, garlic, roasted poppy seeds, almonds, red chillies, cumin, ginger and coriander seeds together in food processor, until pulped and well mixed. Add this mixture to the meat with the salt and flour, mixing everything together well with your hands. The texture of the mixture should be that of soft dough.

Make the filling: finely chop the onions, chillies and ginger. Mix these with the chopped coriander or mint.

Take a small amount of the venison mixture in one hand and mould it into a cup shape. Place a small amount of filling in the centre and mould the venison mixture around the filling. Flatten between the palms of your hands into a small hamburger shape. Repeat until all the mixture is used.

Heat a heavy-based frying pan over medium to high heat and add 15 mls oil. Fry kebabs in batches, turning when one side is well browned. Remove with a fish slice and drain on absorbent paper. Garnish with sliced onion, and sprinkle with lemon juice. Serve with spicy ketchup. Mashed potato can be added to the meat mixture if needed to make it firmer and easier to handle.

Disasters, Discomforts and Emergency Rations

'While, however, even the most enthusiastic adherents of the picnic
will scarcely deny that the sunny hours of preparation that herald
the inevitable downpour when you set out, are the most enjoyable,
or that it is often more pleasurable in reality to think of a picnic,
while steadfastly remaining in your own dining room, than to attend
one, nevertheless the idea is undoubtedly enticing, calls you away
from worries, from the cares and dust of cities.'

(Osbert Sitwell, *Picnics and Pavilions*)

Claudia Roden quotes Georgina Battiscombe in *English Picnics* (1951)
saying the English picnicker is something of a stoic in the face of
our unreliable climate, going on to add that an uncomfortable picnic
may still have the edge over the food available in British hotels and
restaurants. While this may sometimes be the case, there remain all sorts
of good reasons for picnics, not least economic. Roden suggests a certain
masochistic delight taken by the British picnicker in the anticipation of
disaster. Stories of disaster lose nothing in the telling but for those like
me who find little pleasure before, during, or after the event, in a cold,
wet picnic, or the clouds of midges descending to clear a Scottish beach in
record time, some are more amusing than others. There are situations too
that require extreme improvisation and emergency rations and are a good
deal more life-threatening than such small outdoor dramas or those that
enliven Victorian diaries like those of Maud Berkeley.

Picnic Crumbs

Adapted by Flora Fraser, the *Diaries of Maud Berkeley* are jauntily illustrated with her drawings and watercolours and are packed with picnics where minor disaster adds to the entertainment, at least after the event. The picnickers are always accompanied by 'that invaluable aid to every picnic – an umbrella'. Until her marriage, Maud lived on the Isle of Wight, definitely picnic territory but prey to the usual vagaries of the British climate. A 'lovely picnic' on a July sketching excursion with friends had a less satisfactory encore:

> 'Very cold. Heard from Mrs Hatchet, whom we met on the Prom as we were setting out, that there was snow at Portsmouth. Decided in favour of nearby Culver Cliffs for a picnic spot, instead of going further afield. Would never have thought it was high summer. Sat on the sands and shivered our way through cups of tea and toast grilled ineffectually on a pile of sticks. I wore my new hat with the veil, which rather incommoded my attempts to eat and drink.'

On another occasion, 'Mollie Boucher brought a teapot which leaked through the spout, so we were not very adequately served. It was so cold, that, after on an hour or so, we retreated back to Sandown.'

A beach picnic today may be a very different sort of disaster. Digby Anderson describes a family on the beach in *The English at Table* which is at best depressing. 'They had been eating intermittently through the morning and were to continue eating throughout the afternoon' a menu of pizza; bacon and cheese puffs, 'soggy chips covered with tomato ketchup – hamburgers with more ketchup'; 'industrial ice creams with brightly coloured things in them'. Everything was eaten with the fingers except the chips, shovelled into greedy mouths in a 'refined' way with wooden forks. There were bars of chocolate, fizzy drinks and lager for grownups. After 'each instalment of food, one member of the fractured family dutifully took a pile of the polystyrene dishes to throw away in the litter bin. A casual inspection revealed that the dishes had enough chips and ketchup still on them to feed Somalia.'

A bizarre 18th century prank, carefully contrived to shock him to the core, became an unusual picnic disaster for the local vicar at West Wycombe Park, the seat of Sir Francis Dashwood, Postmaster General and founder of the Medmenham Abbey Hellfire Club. Invited by the locally popular Sir Francis to bring his Sunday School for a picnic in the newly laid out gardens, the vicar was taken up the tower by his host, better to observe the delightful view. 'To the minister's astonishment a stream of water shot suddenly from the shrubbery and, from the two red-mounted beds, fountains sprayed out white chalky rivers. They were looking down on the naked body of a woman contrived from the contours of the lawn and plants.' The minister fainted clean away. (Phillippa Pullar, *Consuming Passions*)

Victorian heroism was the regular flip side of major disaster, nicely wrapped in mourning ribbons for the chauvinist and sentimental audience at home. Lord Chelmsford's picnic breakfast at Isandlwana in 1879, at the start of the latest imperialist adventure, if not itself a disaster, was the overly relaxed prelude to a catastrophe for the General and his army, albeit with comforting sidelines of heroism and death at Rorke's Drift, in the best Victorian tradition. The whole Zulu war was an ill-conceived land-grab, the battle lost due to the arrogance of British commanders' assumptions of their strength versus that of natives armed with spears. In the end, the Zulu victors suffered most, crushed by the mechanised weight of imperial vengeance until the Zulu kingdom was shattered.

The picnic is described by Commandant Hamilton-Browne, a colonial officer commanding a contingent of African troops and gives the sense of the total unpreparedness of the English command for what was to follow:

> 'I shall never forget the sight of that peaceful picnic. Here were the staff quietly breakfasting and the whole column scattered over the country! Over there the guns unlimbered, over the hills parties of mounted infantry and volunteers looting the scattered kraals for grain for their horses, a company of the 24th one place and another far away.'

> (Ron Lock and Peter Quantrill, *Zulu Victory*)

Picnic Crumbs

The dramas of a boat trip in another part of the Victorian Empire, a year or two earlier are worthy of Jerome K. Jerome's imagination. In *Life in the Mofussil* the author details his life as assistant magistrate and collector in various stations in Bengal and includes an uncomfortable boat trip en route between Muzufferpore, now Muzaffarpur, in Bihar, to Calcutta.

'We had stuck on a sand bank, covered with only about half a foot of water. Oars and poles were at once put in requisition to shove us off; but the wind drove us on, and though Melville and I worked as hard as the rest, all our efforts were of no use, and we became convinced that we must stick where we were until the wind should moderate. My solar topee (pith hat) was whirled away during the struggle, but that was the only result. As the day passed on, about 6 a.m., I began to feel hungry, and would have given a good deal for a hot cup of coffee and a piece of toast. We looked at our leg of lamb, or rather the small remnant. There was no bread left, and we each had a bit of meat and a sweet biscuit, not a nice mixture, our drink being drawn from the holy Ganges, which trouble-some river we both cursed from the bottom of our hearts.

About midday we felt hungry, and again turned our attention to the remnant of our leg of lamb. To our dismay it had turned green. The damp and muggy heat combined had caused this. With many misgivings we committed it to the stream, to be digested by some river turtle or alligator, and satiated our present pangs with a few sweet biscuits each. Evening came on, but with no change, and we were content to dine off a handful of dry rice, given us by the boatmen; for the wind and rain was such that they could not even attempt to light a fire in our exposed situation.

About ten, a steamer passed us, a long way off; but without taking any notice of our signal of distress, viz., a pair of trousers, belonging to Melville, hauled up the mast. We used these in order to show the steamer people that Europeans were on our country boat. We anathematized this vessel pretty well;

but two hours afterwards, another passed us with the same result, and then our indignation knew no bounds. I mentally composed a tremendous letter to the *Englishman* newspaper on the inhuman conduct of river steamer captains, which, as may be supposed, was never committed to writing. Probably we were not seen, and if we were, I doubt if they could have helped us without considerable risk; for it seemed we had got on a long strip of shallow, to which they were obliged to give a wide berth, and down the side of this a tremendous current was running; and had they stopped near, they would probably have been stranded like ourselves. For all this we were not prepared to make allowances at the time; and to add to our discomfort, the bottom of the boat being now pretty well waterlogged, the rats began to make their appearance in our neighbourhood, and to climb about the thatch roof. We consoled ourselves with the reflection that they would not find much to eat, "Unless it should be our own unhappy persons," I added, with a forced smile; but Melville suggested that it might be the other way, and we should eat them.

(*Life in the Mofussil, Or the Civilian in Lower Bengal*)

According to Calvin W. Schwabe in *Unmentionable Food*, 'Brown Rats and roof rats were eaten openly on a large scale in Paris when the city was under siege during the Franco-Prussian War. Observers likened their taste to both partridge and pork.' Not the only time in history the detested rodents provided sustenance although we are more likely these days to think of rat eating only in the context of a Blackadder joke. In the China of Marco Polo's time, rat was known as 'household deer' (Reay Tannahill, *Food in History*) and a simple recipe for rat, as eaten in certain regions of France, is included in the *Larousse Gastronomique*.

'The flesh of well-nourished rats can be, it seems of good quality, but sometimes with a musky taste. Rats nourished in the wine stores of the Gironde were at one time highly esteemed by the coopers, who grilled them, after having cleaned out and skinned them, on a fire of broken barrels, and seasoned them with a little oil and plenty of shallot. This dish which was then called Cooper's Entrecôte, would be the origin of the Entrecôte à la bordelaise.'

During the 1870 siege of Paris, Choron, the chef at the famous Voisin restaurant, created a menu to celebrate Christmas, the 99th day of the siege, that legend has it included elephant soup made from Castor and Pollux, the two elephants of the zoo; stuffed donkey head, roasted camel, kangaroo stew, rack of bear, leg of wolf, cat garnished with rats, and antelope pie. Not that unusual dishes were entirely alien to the restaurant, saddle of spaniel being served earlier as a meat course. M.F.K. Fisher writes of eating shrimp the first time as an equal test to dishes we find positively barbaric.

'I must eat at least one shrimp, and then die or be sick.' But once tasted things changed so the shrimps, lobsters and all their armoured relations became some 'of the sweetest things in this world to put between my teeth.'

In the middle of Queen Victoria's reign, poor weather, bad harvests and lack of care for the labouring classes affected the rural poor in Britain no less than in more distant parts of her fabulous Empire. At the centre of it all in London, starvation stalked the streets as closely as it did in besieged Paris. *Oliver Twist* was merely an individualised portrait that described the lives of starving children all over the city, where families, with no space, facilities or fuel for cooking in slum tenements, were eating whatever they could afford, scrounge or steal from the streets of the capital. Children in particular suffered the consequences of malnutrition with rickets, tuberculosis and other diseases exacerbated by vitamin deficiency, even the seafarers' scourge, scurvy, came ashore to claim its share of victims. The cheapest food on the streets, other than discarded eel heads, were loaves of bread, or baked potatoes bought from vendors and used to warm frozen hands for as long as possible before eating.

Brewis is poor food for the poor; a crust of bread upon which boiling water is poured, then drained, flavoured with salt and pepper if available and to be eaten with a spoon. Florence White includes a recipe from the 1840s in her collection of traditional foods, *Good Things in England*; it is uncomfortable to imagine the circumstances under which this would be good. Fish became cheap food as the railways brought ever greater supplies from the coast; a bit of fried fish cost a penny; shellfish, kippers and sprats were sold from street barrows. Eels, pea soup, pickled herrings, baked apples, sheep's trotters and muffins were staple street food; penny pies, often made of bad meat disguised with treacle and the strong seasoning that people expected. Sweeney Todd's favourite economy cuts may or may not have been pure fiction. Children bought sweets coloured with arsenic, mercury and lead and the first immigrant Italian ice cream makers sold 'penny licks', often made with dirty milk, cornstarch and lurid colourings.

Worst of all, according to the English women's *Domestic Magazine,* published and edited by Samuel and Isabella Beeton, was the spectacle of boys scouring discarded animal hides by the markets round London Bridge for any piece of meat still adhering to the skin. 'This was poverty's larder – crawling with knife wielding boys "hunting about the hides and flapping them over to get at their fleshy side", swooping down on a tag of meat "like a carrion crow on a worm".' (Kate Coquhoun, *Taste*)

Florence White's collection has an 1870s recipe for eel pie. It may use Thames eels but it sounds like middle class food, the sort of thing enjoyed alfresco by day trippers and the members of the Twickenham Rowing Club on Eel Pie Island, not the cheap food being sold from a stall in the East End of London.

Thames Eel Pie

'Puff pastry; Thames eels 2; hard-boiled eggs; shallots 2 small ones; butter ½oz.; parsley a small faggot chopped; nutmeg; pepper; salt; and sherry 2 glasses; water. For the sauce: butter 2oz.; flour 2oz.; lemon the juice of a whole one. For preparation and cooking 1½ to 2 hours all told.

Skin, cleanse and bone two Thames eels. Cut these in pieces. Chop the shallots; pass them in butter for 5 or 6 minutes and then add to them a small faggot of parsley chopped, with nutmeg, pepper, salt, and two glasses of sherry. In the midst of this place the eels, add enough water to cover them, and set them on the fire to boil. When they have boiled up, take out the pieces of eel and keep them hot. Strain the stock in which they were cooked. Melt the butter and add the flour in the usual way for a foundation sauce. Add the strained stock, beat quite smooth, boil up and finish with the juice of a whole lemon. Arrange the pieces of eel, and quarters of hard-boiled eggs in a pie dish. Pour the sauce over it, and when cold, roof the pie with puff pastry. Bake in a hot oven at first, to raise the pastry and then in a cooler one, one hour all told.'

Eels in any form were highly nutritious at least. The Medical Research Council reported in 1928 that 'the body oil in eels (almost 30% of their whole substance) contains not only vitamin D, but almost as much vitamin A as good cod liver oil – a striking confirmation of the medieval notion that eels have high dietetic value'. And a reason for all the ruins and remains of eel stew ponds in the grounds of ancient monasteries and manors. Eels apparently went out of fashion because it was believed that they had to be skinned alive, not an encouraging idea. I wish we had known as children that eels could be killed instantly by 'piercing the spinal marrow, close to the back part of the skull' – we had usually cut them into several pieces before all motion ceased and they held none of the appeal of other, easier, wild food.

The vinegary cockles, mussels, winkles and whelks of traditional London street stalls are the same as we gathered fresh on the summer beaches of childhood holidays, besides buckets of shrimps collected in nets with a wooden board to push through the sandy bottom of the shallows. Arabella Boxer remembers a friend's story of her nanny eating winkles raw with her hat pin on the beach at Ramsgate before World War 1. Our nanny, at a later date, brought them home to be boiled and then eaten with a large nappy pin. I don't remember that we acquired the taste and I'm none too sure that Nanny really liked them either, they looked too horrible with their lids like blackened finger nails but I can't imagine why we should think them much worse than escargots if we swapped the vinegar for butter and garlic. Cockles are best eaten raw, although they are chewy; mussels, we still gather from the rocks in Scotland on days when we feel energetic enough to scrub them clean or just boil them up with onion, wine and garlic, strain the sauce of grit and pick out the flesh, discarding shells and beards.

Undoubtedly, as children we were spoilt for improvised food and what we would then have seen as emergency rations. A kitchen garden full of ripening peas, pears and peaches in green-houses; the smell of strawberry patches and fruit hidden under leaves; the occasional wasp sting among the raspberry canes and the alien looking hairy gooseberries, rarely perfect and sweet enough to eat raw. Beyond the immediate confines of home, autumn orchards of apples, wild raspberries in the woods and miles of hedgerows full of blackberries, nuts and the bitter sloes and damsons used to make deep red fruit gins and vodkas.

This is instant food for innocents. With all the survival experts we now have on our televisions, let alone the repellent bush dishes served up for contestants in competitive jungle reality programmes, we now know that we can survive anywhere on the occasional stick insect or a small termite nest. We can discover from a whole history of adventure and exploration on sea and land the dos and don'ts of provisioning and staying alive but accidents happen and there are still places in our smaller, better known world, where the best laid plans may fail with no emergency rations to fall back on.

The Donner Party were a disparate group of 81 mid-western farmers and businessmen travelling from Wyoming during the winter of 1846-47 to resettle in California. They paid a high price for badly underestimating the rigours and requirements of the journey; of the original number, 48 survived from groups either left in camp or attempting to keep going and get help. After all their animals had been stolen by Indians, killed for food down to the last pet dog and eaten down to the last piece of stewed hide; they resorted to cannibalism of the dead and of two unfortunate Indian guides who became weak and were considered of little enough account to be killed. Some learned to enjoy human flesh more than others; Lewis Keseberg, the sole survivor at the Donner Lake camp, was found with a pot of human soup and was heard to say that flesh of Mrs Tamsen Donner was the best he had ever tasted. He continued to profess a preference for human brains and liver above other meat which may have contributed to the ultimate failure of his hotel and restaurant business in Sacramento.

The Donner Party Cookbook by anthropologist Terry Alan del Bene gives 19th century recipes for buffalo tongue, antelope and elk that would have been eaten to eke out basic supplies of bacon, beans and hard tack. It includes rather tactless recipes for brains and liver but, aside perhaps from Keseberg, the survivors of the journey were appalled by the means of their survival.

The following account from the *California Star* was the sensationalist tabloid and completely untrue version of events:

> A more shocking scene cannot be imagined, than that witnessed by the party of men who went to the relief of the unfortunate emigrants in the California Mountains. The bones of those who had died and been devoured by the miserable ones that still survived were lying around their tents and cabins. Bodies of men, women and children, with half the flesh torn

from them, lay on every side. A woman sat by the body of her husband, who had just died, eating out his tongue; the heart she had already taken out, broiled, and ate! The daughter was seen eating the flesh of the father - the mother that of her children - children that of father and mother. The emaciated, wild, and ghastly appearance of the survivors, added to the horror of the scene. Language cannot describe the awful change that a few weeks of dire suffering had wrought in the minds of these wretched and pitiable beings. Those who but one month before would have shuddered and sickened at the thought of eating human flesh, or of killing their companions and relatives to preserve their own lives, now looked upon the opportunity by these acts afforded them of escaping the most dreadful of deaths, as a providential interference in their behalf. Calculations were coldly made, as they sat gloomily around their gloomy camp fires, for the next and succeeding meals. Various expedients were devised to prevent the dreadful crime of murder, but they finally resolved to kill those who had the least claims to longer existence. Just at this moment, however, as if by Divine interpolation, some of them died, which afforded the rest temporary relief. Some sunk into the arms of death cursing God for their miserable fate, while the last whisperings of others were prayers and songs of praise to the Almighty.

After the first few deaths, nothing but the one all absorbing thought of individual self-preservation prevailed. The fountains of natural affection were dried up. The cords that once vibrated with connubial, parental and filial affection were rent asunder, and each one seemed resolved without regard to the fate of others to escape from the impending calamity. Even the wild hostile mountain Indians, who once visited their camps, pitied them, and instead of pursuing the natural impulse of their hostile feelings to whites, and destroying them as they could easily have done, divided their own scanty supply of food with them.

So changed had the emigrants become that when the party sent out, arrived with food, some of them cast it aside and seemed to prefer the putrid human flesh that still remained. The day before the party arrived, one of the emigrants took a child of about four years of age in bed with him, and devoured the whole before morning; and the next day eat another about the same age before noon.

It is thought that several more of these unfortunate people might have been saved, but for their determination not to leave their property. Some of them who started in, loaded themselves with their money and other effects to such an extent, that they sunk under them and died on the road. According to the best accounts, forty-three died from starvation. They were principally from the neighbourhood of Independence, Missouri.

In 1972 another story of cannibalism and survival in the most extreme circumstances hit the headlines when 16 people survived ten weeks in the Andes after the plane chartered by an Uruguayan amateur rugby team, 45 passengers crashed in heavy snow. 16 people were eventually rescued including Nando Parrrado and Roberto Canessa, the 'expeditionaries', who walked out of the mountains to reach civilisation in Chile. Once the decision had been made to eat human flesh and the compulsion of starvation made it possible to swallow the strips of meat, it remained a hideous task to slice it from bodies well preserved by the cold and all too recognisably those of their friends and colleagues.

'They had, from necessity, come to eat almost every part of the body. Canessa knew that the liver contained the reserve of vitamins; for that reason he ate it himself and encouraged others to do so until it was set aside for the expeditionaries. Having overcome their revulsion against eating the liver, it was easier to move on to the heart, kidneys and intestines. It was less extraordinary for them to do this than it might have been for a European or a North American, because it was common in Uruguay to eat the intestines and the lymphatic glands of a steer at an asado. The sheets of fat which had been cut from the body were dried in the sun until a crust formed, and then they were eaten by everyone. It was a source of energy and, though not as popular as the meat, was outside the rationing, as were the odd pieces of earlier carcasses which had been left around in the snow and could be scavenged by anyone.'

At night, the boys escaped the horrors of their days, the cold and their cramped and filthy quarters in part of the wrecked plane's fuselage by talking, inevitably about food and in turn describing favourite dishes from their former lives.

'Nogueira, before he died, presented them with cream, meringues, and dulce-de-leche, a thick sweet sauce made with milk and sugar, with a taste between that of condensed milk and caramel cream. Harley, as a winter dish, thought of peanuts and dulce-de-leche coated with chocolate, and, in summer, peanuts and dulce-de-leche ice cream. Algorta had no dish which he could cook himself, but he offered the boys the paella his father sometimes made and his uncle's gnocchi. Parrado could promise the barenkis cooked by his Ukrainian grandmother; and for those who did not know what they were he described these little pancakes filled with cheese, ham, and mashed potatoes. Vizintín, who always spent the summer by the sea near the Brazilian border, described a bouillabaisse, and Methol told him that when they returned he would get Vizintín to show him how to make it.'

Eventually discussion of food was banned as too depressing when faced by reality but the dreams continued.

'Carlitos dreamed of an orange suspended in the air above him. On another occasion he dreamed that a flying saucer came and hovered over the plane. Stairs were lowered and a stewardess came out. He asked her for a strawberry milkshake but was given only a glass of water with a strawberry floating on the top. Roy dreamed that he was in a bakery where biscuits were being shovelled out of the oven. He tried to tell the baker that they were up in the Andes but could not make him understand.'

(Piers Paul Read, *Alive: The Story of the Andes Survivors*)

The Andes survivors were all good Roman Catholics from a college run by the Irish Christian Brothers and were assured on their return that their church accepted that anthropophagy in extremis was not a sin. The hooligan behaviour of the first crusaders, ravaging and pillaging their way to the Holy Land was less easily forgiven by the Turks and Saracens whose spies discovered the bodies of the hungry Christians' captives roasting on spits in their kitchens.

Eating enemies is a not entirely rare event throughout history; to eat friends, however dead and even for survival is a different matter entirely. M.F.K. Fisher follows up her first taste of prawns with a 'dangerously disgusting' oyster; but she goes on to say that she ate, thereafter, oysters whenever she could. This included a 'very bad one in Berne' that her husband assured her would prove to be safe provided she did not die within six hours. 'I did not, although the last hour had me waiting with ill-concealed anxiety, my eyes on the clock and one hand lying expectantly upon the bedside bell'.

She later learned from 'no less an authority than Henri Charpentier' that she should have drunk large quantities of rough red wine, the tannic content of which being a well-known antidote to the acid of a 'rotting mollusc'. She regrets she has not had the opportunity to test this cure, not having since been in 'oysterish places'.

In *Consider the Oyster*, Fisher manages to encourage sympathy for the oyster beyond our fondness for its flesh. 'Life is hard, we say. An oyster's life is worse. She lives motionless, soundless, her own cold ugly shape her only dissipation, and if she escapes the menace of duck-slipper-mussel-Black-Drum-leech-sponge-borer-starfish, it is for man to eat, because of man's own hunger.'

And so we find ourselves weeping with the Walrus as we suck the juice from our oyster shells.

"O Oysters, come and walk with us!"
The Walrus did beseech.
"A pleasant walk, a pleasant talk,
Along the briny beach:
We cannot do with more than four,
To give a hand to each."

The eldest Oyster looked at him,
But never a word he said:
The eldest Oyster winked his eye,
And shook his heavy head –
Meaning to say he did not choose
To leave the oyster-bed.

But four young Oysters hurried up,
All eager for the treat:
Their coats were brushed, their faces washed,
Their shoes were clean and neat –
And this was odd, because, you know,
They hadn't any feet.

Four other Oysters followed them,
And yet another four;
And thick and fast they came at last,
And more, and more, and more –
All hopping through the frothy waves,
And scrambling to the shore.

The Walrus and the Carpenter
Walked on a mile or so,
And then they rested on a rock
Conveniently low:
And all the little Oysters stood
And waited in a row.

Picnic Crumbs

"The time has come," the Walrus said,
"To talk of many things:
Of shoes – and ships – and sealing-wax –
Of cabbages--and kings –
And why the sea is boiling hot –
And whether pigs have wings."

"But wait a bit," the Oysters cried,
"Before we have our chat;
For some of us are out of breath,
And all of us are fat!"
"No hurry!" said the Carpenter.
They thanked him much for that.

"A loaf of bread," the Walrus said,
"Is what we chiefly need:
Pepper and vinegar besides
Are very good indeed –
Now if you're ready, Oysters dear,
We can begin to feed."

"But not on us!" the Oysters cried,
Turning a little blue.
"After such kindness, that would be
A dismal thing to do!"
"The night is fine," the Walrus said.
"Do you admire the view?

"It was so kind of you to come!
And you are very nice!"
The Carpenter said nothing but
"Cut us another slice:
I wish you were not quite so deaf –
I've had to ask you twice!"

"It seems a shame," the Walrus said,
"To play them such a trick,
After we've brought them out so far,
And made them trot so quick!"
The Carpenter said nothing but
"The butter's spread too thick!"

"I weep for you," the Walrus said:
"I deeply sympathize."
With sobs and tears he sorted out
Those of the largest size,
Holding his pocket-handkerchief
Before his streaming eyes.

"O Oysters," said the Carpenter,
"You've had a pleasant run!
Shall we be trotting home again?'
But answer came there none –
And this was scarcely odd, because
They'd eaten every one.

(Lewis Carroll, *Through the Looking Glass*)

School Food

At Hurstpierpoint College in Sussex, on Ascension Day, the whole school walks through the village and up Wolstonbury ('Danny') hill to sing the 17th century *Hymnus Eucharistus* which is followed by the gift of Lowe's Dole, £1 to each boy who had served in chapel during the last year, in the choir, as a sacristan or an organist, from the gift of the first headmaster. More prosaically, the boys then hurry back to school as fast as their legs can carry them to spend the money on sweets in the school tuck shop.

Every religious feast has its food traditions and many of them have been absorbed into the traditions of schools founded in the name of one or other faith. Ascension Day is rather apparently associated with upward flight, suggesting to the leadership of a Christian educational foundation an excuse for a healthy uphill scramble followed by a celebratory communal picnic. Tradition suggests that the business of vertical take-off should be commemorated with feathered food and fowl, pigeon, pheasant or even crow have made their way onto Ascension Day menus. German chefs make bird shaped pastries which sound a good deal more pleasing than crow, even covered with a nice flaky piecrust in a rook pie. Bird pie, including one in which the birds, like the four and 20 blackbirds, remained alive to fly out when the pastry was cut open, was a Tudor and Stuart favourite but one more usually seen at Christmas. There was, may still be, a tradition that some loyal officer of state should send a fully cooked pie containing a great number of birds, four and 20 woodcock for instance, to the monarch at that time of year.

Picnic Crumbs

I don't remember any picnicking attached to the stiff walk up neighbouring Hambledon or Hod hills on Ascension Day when I was at prep school in Dorset. Later, at public school in Wiltshire, we followed a whole school general knowledge test in the morning, which was taken very seriously indeed, with an outing in buses to the Marlborough Downs and a gentler stroll to the 19th century white horse above the village of Alton Barnes. Picnics came always in individual paper bags and held few surprises although they seemed interesting enough in days when school food still meant Heinz style spaghetti in tomato sauce, banana custard and toad in the hole and the dining room had the typical school smell of antique boiled brassicas. Ex-pupils a few years older than me remember special pastries for Ascension Day picnics with circles of red, yellow and green jam, not surprisingly called traffic lights.

Special pastries for Ascension Day in this country, not so far as anyone knows bird-shaped, were called Rammalation Cakes and usually eaten at the end of the ceremony of beating the parish bounds on the Rogation Days immediately preceding Ascension Day in the old church calendar. Rogation days were associated with the blessing of crops and prayers for a good harvest and the cakes were accompanied by Gangen beer. The etymology of both names has been as completely lost as their recipes. I rather doubt that Rammalation Cakes looked like traffic lights but the traffic lights may have had some underlying symbolism, unknown to us but dreamt up in the imagination of our deeply religious and slightly strange headmistress.

Other school picnics, speech days, parents' days and sports days, are part of unchanging traditions of celebration of the lives of long dead founders. Depending on the age of the school, some a lot deader than others. They are often a good enough excuse for pupils to get blind drunk on the vast supplies of alcohol brought by parents keen to get through the whole thing feeling as little pain as possible and can end in recrimination and retribution when things get out of hand. They are also the time when most parents discover that, however grand the school and barring a very few others who are already friends, all the rest are odd, bad or mainly boring. After experiencing about 30 years of such occasions in a great number of schools, I know this to be the case. It is also inevitable that you will suddenly make friends with those you have shunned for years just as your child is leaving. There is comfort in good food as well as alcohol.

My summer school picnic has become as standardised by family demand as the unending cold chicken of travellers' picnics through the years but that does make it very easy too. This is it with the occasional inclusion of an inelegant but good egg mayonnaise without which a picnic is not complete for my husband.

Really good crisps with taramasalata and yoghurt dip; cold asparagus with mayonnaise or vinaigrette; a bowl of cherry tomatoes on their branches; another of cherries or grapes; a great many sticky chipolata sausages, cooked in honey or treacle with grain mustard and packed up in silver foil in plastic boxes wrapped with picnic rugs to arrive still warm; small pieces of chicken marinated overnight in soy, mirin, ginger, garlic, cooked in the oven in the marinade and wrapped like the sausages; lettuce leaves to wrap the teriyaki chicken with cucumber fingers, sliced spring onion and, oddly, much loved *hoisin* sauce; phyllo pasties or samosas of spiced duck or other minced or curried meat; possibly soup, gazpacho or hot tomato, depending on the weather; a ripe brie, butter and a French loaf or two; assorted cakes, biscuits or chocolates, definitely not homemade. Then there are paper plates, paper napkins, plastic glasses in sizes to suit wine or soup, plastic spoons and forks; a handful of proper sharp knives; a corkscrew; a bottle opener; wet wipes; a bin bag and another bag for dirty non-disposables. The food is mostly packed in bowls and dishes balanced in some sort of non-refrigerated box. Things like wine, beer and butter that need to stay cold go in the usual insulated affairs or plastic boxes filled with ice. The drink is champagne, perhaps; the makings of Pimms, probably; and the palest pink wine, definitely; plus lager, coke or lemonade; cider and water.

Constance Spry says that, 'Hungry boys like hot dogs; frankfurters poached in boiling water for seven minutes, drained, and put into a soft fresh roll or bap buttered, lavishly spread with French mustard and given a rub of garlic; or a grilled chipolata in a French roll', so perhaps that is why my sausages always disappear so fast.

Bryanston School Spicy Plum Chutney

900g plums; 450g onions, peeled and finely chopped; 450g sultanas; 900g white granulated sugar; 1.2 litres distilled malt vinegar or wine vinegar; 1 rounded teaspoon ginger; 2 round teaspoons mustard seeds; ½ rounded teaspoon curry powder; ½ rounded teaspoon cinnamon; ½-1 level teaspoon ground cloves; 25g salt.

Stone the plums and chop into 5mm pieces. Put all the ingredients including the plums into a wide stainless-steel pan. Simmer gently over a low-medium heat until the sugar has dissolved and the mixture is soft and pulpy, stirring frequently. Cook uncovered for approximately 1½-2 hours until very thick and dark brown and reduced to about 1/3 of original volume. Stir frequently towards the end of the cooking time to avoid the chutney burning as it becomes more concentrated. Pot in sterilised jars, cover immediately and label. Store in dry, airy cupboard or larder and allow to mature for four weeks before using.

M.F.K. Fisher remembers American school picnics in the late 20s or early 30s for festivals like Easter and Old Girls' Day when the school cook, an otherwise unpleasing character, showed off her remarkable culinary skill to best advantage. She must have been an extraordinary woman who not only fed her charges four times a day 'with probably the best institutional food in America' but also managed to do so under circumstances when normal domestic irritations like flooded basements were overtaken by high drama. Even the head boy committing 'double murder and hara kiri' on Good Friday failed to delay or diminish a good meal.

Old Girls' Day meant wearing gym bloomers without stockings and a lavish picnic on the sea shore below the school in which the most memorable ingredients were 'the hot crisp halves of young chickens, stiff and tempting' eaten in the fingers with abandon and in as great a quantity as anyone could manage.

School picnics also mean packed lunches and, oh dear, what a vexed question they have become now we are so excessively and changeably informed on proper food for growing children. Older books called things like *Healthy Food for Kids* or, supposedly more infant friendly, Winnie the Pooh's 'Healthy Snacks', an oxymoron of a title if ever there was, suggest interesting ways to serve up peanut butter among other healthy options that are now completely banned from class rooms due to ALLERGIES. Peanuts are a regular part of the diet given to undernourished children in developing countries; they are cheap, packed with protein, vitamins and minerals and could be called life rather than deathnuts, which is another name they go by, though it appears to pre-date allergies and anaphylactic shock. The latest view is that the peanuts used in developing countries are the real unprocessed deal and it is in the processing that allergens appear; this probably does not come as a blinding shock to most of us.

Other expectedly healthy foods can also cause anaphylaxis – most nuts; cow's milk; egg; soya; wheat; seeds; seafood; mustard; fish; sulphite food preservatives that are found in foods and drinks from Sauvignon Blanc to sausages and, strangely, celery. Allergies are also caused by meat, sesame seeds, different vegetables and on and on... So, what do you put in a child's packed lunch these days when almost everything that used to be healthy might now make another child ill? No peanut butter, egg, or sardine sandwiches one supposes, not even in gluten free bread, no celery sticks that my children used to eat all the time. According to the books, whatever the food is, it has to be packed in appetising little packages in the Disneyfied lunch box that will make the little darling jump for joy as well as giving it the energy to get through the afternoon.

A 1985 pre-allergy panic book offers savoury and sweet sandwiches full of various nutty mixtures, among other dainty dishes that would keep you up all night making them. Somehow there is no cohesion and no standard dish that might appeal to most children as seems more to be the case in countries with a more clearly defined national cuisine than ours. Maybe I'm wrong, but I doubt any of my children would have eaten a sandwich made of low-fat curd cheese mashed with cold peas and mint and filled with thinly sliced cold lamb, let alone tongue, margarine and redcurrant jelly. More child-pleasing ideas from the same publication, involving the sweet and sticky such as chocolate spread, would no longer be at all the thing during an obesity epidemic and a steady rise in childhood diabetes and I can't say that chocolate spread ever seemed an ideal lunch dish.

This 'Children's Favourite' ticks most of the health and allergen boxes I should imagine, notwithstanding the ketchup, but is it going to be eaten from its small plastic bowl with a snap on lid by some child more interested in play than food?

Children's Favourite

- 2 tablespoons diced cooked chicken
- 1-2 tablespoons cooked peas or green beans
- 1-2 tablespoons cooked sweetcorn or baked beans
- 1 small sliced carrot, cooked or raw
- 1 tablespoon tomato ketchup
- 1 tablespoon plain yoghurt

Mix altogether.

I have unpacked an awful lot of uneaten lunch boxes in my time and I think this might have been in one of them. Perhaps all children now are better brainwashed to eat healthily unless they are the obese ones of course but one can't help but feel that hours spent constructing terribly healthy little bits of this and that are more to make parents feel better than anything else. Really children like food that is quick and easy to eat and tastes right; usually straightforward sandwiches in some hopefully non-allergenic form, fruit ready to eat, carrot sticks maybe, raisins or similar and fruity yoghurts or fromage frais. Depressingly they would probably prefer crisps, chocolate and their sandwich bread white and soggy, whether we like it or not.

Children's packed lunches in other countries often sound so much better than ours although they too are increasingly adulterated by the crisps and fast food options available all over the world. In Asia particularly, foods that are part of everyday cooking seem to lend themselves well to the packed lunch. Japan children might have *onigir*i, rice balls, or *norimake*, seaweed rolls of rice and something savoury or the same bento boxes as adults. These may take time in the making but will use similar ingredients to those being cooked for the family dinner; rice, omelette strips, cooked meat or fish, cooked or pickled vegetables and umeboshi, Japanese pickled apricot.

Madhur Jaffrey's description of children on a school expedition to the temples at Mahabalipuram in Tamil Nadu eating their packed lunches from banana leaves and tiffin carriers makes one hungry to read it. It somehow sounds so sophisticated and civilised compared with the plastic boxes but these days they have taken over India too.

> 'Having inspected, with required awe, the carved granite temples built at Mahabalipuram on Tamil Nadu's eastern shore some one thousand two hundred years ago, they are about to embark upon the exceedingly pleasant business of eating their lunches.
> One girl opens up a newspaper bundle to reveal a second package made out of banana leaf. She smooths out the newspaper with her tiny hands, transforming it into an instant tablecloth. Then she undoes the second package to reveal two spongy *idlis* shaped like small flying saucers. To make them, a batter of ground, parboiled rice and split peas (*urad dal*) was left to ferment overnight. In the morning, when it was a mass of tiny, seething bubbles, it was poured into a whole tree of madeleine-like moulds and steamed. The small, fluffy cakes that formed in the vapour could, of course, have been eaten instantly with a coconut chutney but, for the child going on a trip, they were dipped into oil to prevent them from turning sour in the hot sun and then dipped again into *milagai podi,* a glorious mixture of roasted and coarsely ground seasonings

such as sesame seeds, coriander seeds, red chillies and split peas.

A second child, her braided hair tied up in two loops with crisp ribbons, has opened up her tiffin-carrier and is using a spoon to tuck into yoghurt rice – or curd rice, as they say here when speaking in English. The preparation of this dish has been nothing short of ingenious. In the morning, freshly cooked, slightly soft rice was mixed with milk and a few spoons of yoghurt. Then the combination was seasoned with mustard seeds, *urad dal* and red chillies, popped quickly in hot oil, as well as fresh bits of green coriander, green chillies and ginger. As the child peered at massive elephants carved out of granite rocks or monkeys caught in playful poses on a stone frieze, the contents of her tiffin-carrier were going through a metamorphosis. The same heat that might have soured the first child's *idlis* had precautions not been taken, were working to the benefit of the second child by turning the milk in her container into yoghurt. A dish that was half-prepared when the child left home in the early morning was, by noon, the glorious, cooling, soothing, perky rice salad of the South, called *thayir saadam* in Tamil Nadu and *masuru anna* in Karnataka.' (*A Taste of India*)

The scarcity of interesting food at boarding schools in the past encouraged the creative and the naughty to add excitement by eating the wrong things in the wrong place at the wrong time. Stealing bread to cook over a smoky fire in the woods above the games pitches or, the usual climax to the term at Mallory Towers and other fictional schools, the midnight feast. I remember some very strange ones; purloined champagne that blew its top under the covers of someone's bed, a lot of pink and white sugar mice and slabs of cheddar cheese that were improbably sold by the ounce off an enormous block in the local off licence, our nearest out of bounds shop. Boarders these days are hardly likely to bother with such innocent rule-breaking shenanigans when they have good enough food in dining rooms, sixth form coffee shops, kitchens in their boarding houses and regular supplies of food from local shopping trips and days out. When we were incarcerated juniors, the older girls, who were allowed into the local town, brought back digestive biscuits to sell in the lower school for five pence each, whole Mars bars were worth impossible amounts and were usually profitably sold off in minutely measured slices at more affordable prices.

My son's traditional prep school provided the child actors and the setting for the film, *A Feast at Midnight,* starring Christopher Lee as a vampirish Latin teacher and Robert Hardy as a suitably tweedy headmaster. The arrival of a new boy, Magnus, who detests the all-important team games but loves food, leads to the creation of the 'Scoffers Club' dedicated to the secret cooking of boy fantasy puddings. In a rebellion against the excessively healthy school regime, huge chocolate cakes and crackling crème brulees are constructed in the deserted night-time kitchens using recipes supplied by Magnus' gourmet father. From the child actors' point of view the best part was creeping about their real school at night and the finale, a food fight on a spectacular scale in the school dining room.

The best fictional school feast for me is in *A Little Princess*, Frances Hodgson Burnett's undoubtedly sentimental but quite delicious story of Sara Crewe, whose pampered existence at Miss Minchin's Select Seminary for Young Ladies comes to a dramatic end when her wealthy expatriate father's speculative investment in diamond mines fails and he dies in India of jungle fever. Sara's imagination contrives to transform her new existence of miserable servitude at Miss Minchin's hands and the cold in her dirty garret into the life of a princess imprisoned in the Bastille where she draws her fellow prisoner, Becky, the little scullery maid, into her magical dreams of food, warmth and comfort. The magic begins to come true when another 'Indian Gentleman', Mr Carrisford, moves into the house next door to the seminary with his servant, Ram Dass, to whom Sara speaks in Hindustani, her childhood language, when his monkey escapes across the rooftop into her attic window. Things start to change for Sarah when she falls asleep after a scene with the terrible Miss Minchin, who has caught her remaining friends among the pupils visiting her room.

"'Suppose there was a bright fire in the grate, with lots of little dancing flames,' she murmured. 'Suppose there was a comfortable chair before it – and suppose there was a small table near, with a little hot – hot supper on it. And suppose' – as she drew her thin coverings over her – 'suppose this was a beautiful soft bed, with fleecy blankets and large downy pillows. Suppose – suppose –' and her very weariness was good to her, for her eyes closed and she fell fast asleep.

When she awakened it was rather suddenly, and she did not know that any particular thing had called her out of her sleep. The truth was, however, that it was a sound which had called her back – a real sound – the click of the skylight as it fell in closing after a lithe white figure which slipped through it and crouched down close by upon the slates of the roof – just near enough to see what happened in the attic, but not near enough to be seen.

Of course it was a dream. She felt as if warm, delightful bedclothes were heaped upon her. She could actually *feel* blankets, and when she put out her hand it touched something exactly like a satin-covered-eider-down quilt. She must not awaken from this delight – she must be quite still and make it last.

Her eyes opened in spite of herself. And then she actually smiled – 'Oh I *haven't* awakened, I am dreaming yet.' She knew it must be a dream, for if she were awake such things could not – could not be.

This is what she saw. In the grate there was a glowing, blazing fire; on the hob was a little brass kettle hissing and boiling; spread upon the floor was a thick, warm crimson rug; before the fire a folding-chair, unfolded, and with cushions on it; by the chair a small folding-table, covered with a white cloth, and upon it spread small covered dishes, a cup, a saucer, a teapot; on the bed were new warm coverings and a satin-covered down quilt. At the foot a curious wadded silk robe, a pair of quilted slippers and some books. The room of her dream seemed changed into fairyland.

She took her candle and stole out of her own room and into Becky's, and stood by her bedside.

'Becky, Becky!' she whispered as loudly as she dared. 'Wake up!'

Imagine if you can, what the rest of the evening was like. How they crouched by the fire, which blazed and leaped and made so much of itself in the little grate. How they removed the covers of the dishes and found rich, hot , savoury soup, which was a meal in itself, and sandwiches, and toast and muffins enough for both of them.

It cannot be denied that as they sat before the blazing fire and ate the nourishing, comfortable food, they felt a kind of rapturous awe, and looked into each other's eyes with something like doubt.

'Do you think,' Becky faltered once, in a whisper - 'do you think it could melt away, miss? Hadn't we better be quick?' And she hastily crammed her sandwich into her mouth. If it was only a dream, kitchen manners would be overlooked."

(Frances Hodgson Burnett, *A Little Princess* 1905)

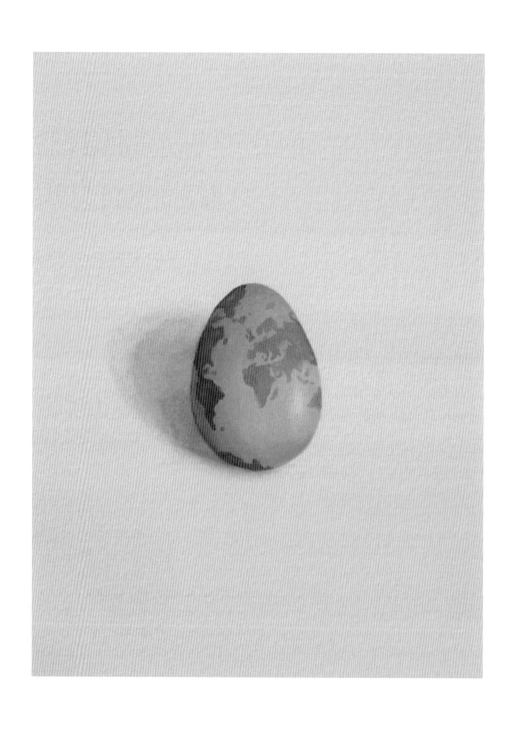

A Finale of Sandwiches
and Filling Stuff

In the end a sandwich makes the best and easiest picnic or packed lunch, suiting all circumstances and eventualities with some fitting filling or other. Lord Sandwich's mythical first at the gaming tables; later, more elegant with drinks at the bridge table; the mighty doorsteps of cottage loaf, slab of cheese and dollop of pickle for the outdoor worker; the individually crafted creation of the boutique city sandwich shop eaten at the computer screen; the too cold constructions of supermarkets and coffee shop chains; the smoked salmon in opera or ballet intervals; do-it-yourself baps and rolls for country picnics with ham and rough pâtés; holiday breakfast bacon and mustard; and the unchanging pleasure of elegantly tiny crustless teatime sandwiches, seldom fitted in to hurried daily schedules except as rare hotel or weekend treats. The brown, white, pitta, baguette, organic, gluten free, light as a feather slimming, soda, country, sourdough, ciabatta, walnut, milk, and olive oil bread choices. The no butter, yes butter, margarines and spreads, mayonnaise and mustard decisions to be made. The salad dressed or undressed, the American crammed, the French ham roll, the prosciutto stuck between the teeth, the hatefulness of sweet corn in it all disaster. The honey and the hummus, sardines and salmon paste, dressed crabs and Dublin prawns, with rocket, lettuce, baby spinach and mustard and cress, tomato, not cucumber, soaking through the spongy bread, toasted bread and grilled cheese, topless in Scandinavia, wrapped in South America. You can't go wrong with a sandwich.

'The proper accompaniment of a sandwich is not the schoolboy's ginger beer or railway station coffee, but a glass of champagne, or some of the excellent white French wines which at present are cheaper than beer.

If a busy City millionaire can lunch on sandwiches and desires nothing better, why shouldn't sandwich lunches be popular in Mayfair? There is as much art in making sandwiches as in preparing a French menu, and many hostesses who offer their friends indifferently cooked pretentious lunches would, with far less trouble, gain an epicurean reputation if they were content with the simplicity of wine and sandwiches.'

(Hilda Leyel and Olga Hartley, *The Gentle Art of Cookery*)

'All I shall say, then, is that the food of the perfect picnic should be near the earth and of it, without being lethal or botulistic, should include, crushed between the Stonehenge boulders that sometimes do service for bread, none of those slimy layers of paste like something out of *The Ancient Mariner*.'

(Osbert Sitwell)

Sandwich's Sandwich (The very first)

From *Cookery Recipes by Famous People for Returned British Prisoners of War Association Cookery Book* to which the then Earl of Sandwich contributed this:

Cut two slices of bread of medium thickness, triangular in shape; spread each with butter on one side, putting the buttered sides together. Insert between them a slice of cold meat, beef, mutton, ham, chicken or other bird, or sardine. Add, to taste, a little salt or mustard or sliced pickle – as an alternative or addition mustard, cress or salad. Press firmly together.

A

Asparagus Rolls

> Cooked Asparagus tips dipped in Plain Dutch sauce and rolled in thinly sliced buttered wholemeal bread. For the Dutch Sauce: a large gravy spoonful of white sauce heated in a pan with 4 egg yolks, a little grated nutmeg, 2oz butter, salt and pepper; stir briskly on the fire; pass through a hair sieve; keep warm and add a little tarragon vinegar or lemon juice before using. These can be varied with savoury or plain seasoned butters.
>
> (Florence White, *Good Things in England*)

B

Banana Hallucinations (suggested by Claudia Roden)

> 'As children in Egypt we were amazed to see our English school friends mashing bananas with thick cream and putting them into a sandwich with a very thin layer of strawberry jam'.

Did English children in Egypt really eat these? We used to have plain sliced bananas in brown bread and butter which were delicious.

> 'Sandwiches for afternoon tea, or any occasion where they will come in contact with gloved fingers, should be left perfectly plain on the outside, but when they may be eaten with a fork some pretty effects may be produced by decorating them with variously-coloured chaudfroid sauces. Or they may be decorated with cold aspic jelly, and garnished with lobster coral, Krona pepper, parsely, cress, small salad, hard-boiled egg, etc'
>
> (Mrs Beeton, *Household Management*)

Eating sandwiches with a fork seems to reduce the whole concept somewhat.

C

Caviare Sandwiches

'Prepare some thin slices of bread, spread them lightly with Russian caviar, sprinkle with lemon-juice and a little cayenne. Have ready an equal number of slice of bread and creamed butter, cover, press lightly together, trim, and cut into square, triangular, or finger-shaped pieces. These sandwiches may be varied by using lobster, prawn, or shrimp butter, any of which flavours combine agreeably with that of caviar.'

(Mrs Beeton)

D

Delhi Sandwich (Leyel and Hartley)

'Six anchovies, three sardines, one teaspoonful of chutney, one egg, one ounce of butter, one small teaspoonful of curry powder.

Free the sardines and anchovies from bones. Pound them with the seasonings, the chutney and butter. Beat up the yolk of the egg and stir this in, with a pinch of cayenne. Heat the mixture stirring it into a smooth paste.

This is excellent spread between toast. The toast should be made in rather thick slices, split in two, and the soft sides buttered.'

E

Epicurean Butter

8 anchovy fillets; yolks of 2 hard-boiled eggs; 4oz (115g) softened unsalted butter; ½ teaspoon Dijon mustard; 12 crushed green peppercorns; 2 small gherkins, finely chopped;

1 level teaspoon finely chopped capers; 1 level tablespoon finely chopped chives; 1 level tablespoon finely chopped tarragon or chervil; a squeeze of lemon juice; 8 slices fresh thin wholemeal or white bread from a large loaf.

Blend anchovy fillets in a food processor with the crumbled egg yolks, butter and mustard or pound the ingredients in a bowl. Mix in the peppercorns, gherkins, capers, chives and tarragon. Add lemon juice to taste. Spread on crustless bread slices to make sandwiches.'

(Readers Digest, *Creative Cooking and Entertaining*)

F

Fish Sandwiches

Cut some slices of brown bread and butter and put a layer of nice cold fish. Spread this over with gherkin, then tartar sauce, and over this lay some thin slices of cold hard boiled egg, and a sprinkling of shredded lettuce leaves on top, then press the top slice of bread, and butter well down and cut into diamond shapes.'

(The Anglo-Indian Cuisine)

'Sandwiches of thinnest gruyere between biscuits, or bread spread with green butter are excellent, and this is easily made and welcome in winter and summer, giving variety to the cheese course'

G

Green Butter (Agnes Jekyll, Kitchen Essays)

A ¼lb good fresh butter. A couple of handfuls of spinach, boiled, drained and passed through a hair sieve, the pulp obtained saved in a bowl. Bone and wipe off the oil of 6 anchovies, pass through sieve and save pulp. Mince finely a tablespoonful of capers. Colour the butter first by working in the spinach greening, then add the other ingredients and turn into a block or an attractive small mould, or use for sandwiches after hardening in the ice box.

H

Hard-boiled Eggs

'Hard-boiled eggs would make a good sandwich if it were not for their untidiness in consumption; as it is, an egg in one hand and bread and butter, or a sandwich, in the other is the best way to deal with them. But eggs are very valuable in many of the mixtures for placing between slices of bread and butter.'
(The Pleasures of the Table, Meals Sub-Jove)

I

Indian Sandwiches

Cut the breast of a roast fowl or pheasant in very small square pieces, also about four ounces of tongue or lean ham, four anchovies washed and filleted; mix well with the chicken, and put it into a stew-pan with two spoonfuls of velouté sauce, a dessert-spoonful of curry paste, half a teaspoonful of chutnee, the juice of half a lemon, and a little salt and pepper. Boil for a few minutes on the stove, mixing well. Have ready prepared some thin slices of bread cut with a circular cutter, as many as you require for your dish, fry them in oil of a bright yellow, drain them on a napkin, and place half of them on a baking-sheet covered with clean paper; spread a thick layer of the above preparation on each, and cover with another crouton. Next grate four ounces of parmesan, cheese, mix it into a paste with butter, divide it into as many parts as there are sandwiches, roll each into a round ball and place one on the top of each sandwich. About ten minutes before serving put them into the oven; let them be thoroughly heated; pass a red hot salamander over them; dish on a napkin and serve.'

(Lady Harriet St Clair, *Dainty Dishes*)

J

Jam

1 kilo strawberries (net weight); 750g sugar; 1dl water.

Put the sugar in a pan with the water; let it dissolve and cook to the ball stage (240° F), taking care to skim well.

Put the strawberries, stalks removed, in the sugar. Keep the pan on the side of the fire for a few minutes.

When the juice from the strawberries has thinned the sugar to a syrupy consistency, drain the fruit through a silk strainer.

Cook the syrup again in the pan until it reaches 240° once more.

Put the strawberries back in the pan and cook for 5 or 6 minutes, just to the point at which the jam reaches the jelling stage (350° F). Finish in the usual way.

(Larousse Gastronomique)

K

Kipper Cheese Paste

As Grouse cheese paste. 'Pound 6 oz of cold grouse debris with the same amount of gruyere cheese, add 2 oz of butter, season with salt and cayenne pepper and pass through the sieve. Finish with two tablespoons of double cream. Should gruyere cheese not be available some new Cheshire or Cheddar may be substituted. You will find that, if you make this paste into a suitable sixed block and keep it in a cold place, you will be able to cut slices from it, arrange them on toast, frill them and serve as an excellent savoury.
(William Heptinstall, *Hors D'Oeuvre and Cold Table*)

L

Lady Llanover's Rice Bread

'In 1867, Lady Llanover writing in Good Cookery gave a detailed description of the preparation of food cooked to be taken on a journey from South Wales to London. For the sandwiches two plump chickens were roasted, and rice bread specially baked the previous day. Lady Llanover held that rice bread was by far the best kind for sandwiches, and preserved the moistness of the chicken meat as well as its own.
Rice is now so expensive that using it for bread can scarcely be called an economy, except in so far as it does give exceptional keeping qualities to the loaf. It is hard to describe the flavour of rice bread: until it has been tried, it is also difficult to believe how delicious it is.'
(Elizabeth David, *English Bread and Yeast Cookery*)

M

Mosaic Sandwiches

Cut heart shapes out of thin slices of white and dark bread trimmed of their crust. Spread half the brown hearts and half the white hearts with butter and filling. Using a tiny heart cutter, cut a small heart from each of the remaining bread hearts and cover the sandwiches, the fillings will show through. Diamonds, stars, circles or any assortment of attractive shapes may be used.

(*The Gourmet Cookbook*)

N

Nan's Connyonny

'My Nan ate connyonny sandwiches, they were a Liverpool speciality, condensed milk spread between two slices of bread. She gave us sugar sandwiches and called a packed lunch a carryon. We ate chip butties too – still do sometimes and food of any sort was known as scran.'

(Liz from Liverpool)

O

Offula

The sandwich was not first hit upon by the earl in the reign of George III, as the Romans were very fond of sandwiches, called by them, *offula*.

'It is curious to think of this dashing edible, the sustenance of lords at their dice coming to the support nowadays of school treats, business girls, stock-jobbers, and debutantes dewy with primal innocence. But happily few are aware of its origin, and fewer still brood upon its inventor. He walked with a shamble, he was supremely unlucky at cards, and denied by Fate even the compensatory good fortune in love. Miss Ray, his delightful actress mistress, was shot as she left her theatre one night by an amorous clergyman. I know, as has been explained in another place, nothing whatever about the Romans; therefore I begin and end my introduction of the sandwich with this brief note upon its eponym, and ignore the repulsively named offula as entirely as I may.'

(Helen Simpson, *The Cold Table*)

P

Pumpkin and Tomato Chutney

'It is not generally known that pumpkin can make an excellent chutney, rich and dark. The recipe below produces a mixture with a taste which is spicy but not too sharp; the pumpkin slices retain something of their shape, and shine translucently through the glass jars.

Ingredients are a 2½ lb piece of pumpkin (gross weight), 1lb of ripe tomatoes, ½lb onions, 2oz. of sultanas, ¾lb each of soft dark brown sugar and white caster sugar, 2 tablespoons of salt, 2 scant teaspoons each of ground ginger, black peppercorns and allspice berries, 2 cloves of garlic, 1¼ pints of white, red or rosé wine vinegar or cider vinegar.

Peel the pumpkin, discard the seed and the cottony centre. Slice, then cut into pieces roughly 2 inches wide and long and ½ inch thick. Pour boiling water over the tomatoes, skin and slice them. Peel and slice the onions and the garlic.

Put all solid ingredients, including spices (crush the peppercorns and allspice berries in a mortar) and sugar, in your preserving pan. (For chutneys always use heavy aluminium, never untinned copper jam pans.) Add vinegar. Bring gently to the boil, and then cook steadily, but not at a gallop until the mixture is jammy. Skim from time to time, and towards the end of the cooking, which will take altogether about 50 minutes, stir very frequently. Chutney can be a disastrous sticker if you don't give it your full attention during the final stages.

This is a long-keeping chutney, but like most chutneys, it is best if cooked to a moderate set only; in other words it should still be a little bit runny; if too solid it will quickly dry up.

Ladle into pots, which should be filled right to the brim. When cold cover with rounds of waxed paper, and then with Porosan skin or a double layer of thick greaseproof paper. Transparent covers which let in the light are not suitable for chutney.

The yield from these quantities will be approximately 3½lb; and although it may be a little more extravagant as regards fuel and materials, I find chutney cooked in small batches more satisfactory than when produced on a large scale.'

(Elizabeth David, *Spices, Salt and Aromatics in the English Kitchen*)

Quince Paste (Dulce de Membrillo)

Peel and core 2kg quinces. Roughly chop the flesh and put it in a heavy pan with the water. Bring the water to the boil, turn down to a simmer, cover and leave to cook for 30 minutes. At the end of this time you will have purée. Process or sieve to remove lumps. Weigh the purée and stir in 250g of sugar per 500g of pulp.

Return the sugared pulp to the pan and simmer for 45 minutes uncovered. At the end of this time pour the mixture into a lightly greased oblong baking tray, to the depth of about 2.5cm. Leave to cool and when it is completely cold cut into squares. Store in a tin wrapped in greaseproof paper. (Quince, Damson and other fruit cheeses were well known in old English cookery but the Moorish or Spanish versions are the ones we see now to be eaten with hard cheese, especially Spanish Manchego.)

(Sarah Woodward, *Moorish Food*)

R

Reality Sandwiches

> *On Burrough's Work*
> *The method must be purest meat*
> *and no symbolic dressing,*
> *actual visions and actual prisons*
> *as seen then and now*
>
> *Prisons and vision presented*
> *with rare descriptions*
> *corresponding exactly to those*
> *of Alcatraz and Rose*
>
> *A naked lunch is natural to us*
> *we eat reality sandwiches.*
> *But allegories are so much lettuce.*
> *Don't hide the madness.*
> San Jose 1954
> (Allen Ginsberg, *Reality Sandwiches*)

S

Soho Sandwiches

Ingredients: White bread; powdered Parmesan cheese; butter; Italian vermouth.

Toast on one side only very thin slices of bread. Make a paste of the powdered Parmesan and vermouth. Butter the untoasted side of the bread and spread the paste on this. Put two pieces together or cover the paste with crisp salted potato crisps.

Note. The cheese must be powdered not merely grated (*The Cold Table*)

T

Terrine Maison

6 rashers streaky bacon/½ lb pig's liver/1 small onion/1 clove of garlic/½lb sausage meat/½lb minced fat pork/2 chopped hard-boiled eggs/1 teaspoon chopped herbs/½lb veal or game/seasoning/bayleaf.

Take a small earthenware terrine. Line across the bottom and sides with bacon. Mince the liver with the onion and garlic and add to the sausage meat and pork. Season well, add the chopped eggs and herbs, and put a layer of this farce on the bottom of the terrine.

Cut the veal or game into fine strips; arrange this in layers with the rest of the farce until the terrine is full. The top layer must be of farce and the bayleaf should be placed on top. Put the lid on and seal round the edge with a paste of flour and water. Stand in a roasting-tin full of water and cook in a moderate oven for 1 to 1½ hours. Take out, remove the lid, and put a weight on the top (of not more than 2lb). Leave until the next day, then fill up the sides of the terrine with good jellied stock. Leave until quite set and then turn out.

U

Udder Sandwich?

'Take a young Udder and lard it with great lard, being seasoned with nutmeg, pepper, cloves and mace, boil it tender, and being cold wrap it in a caul of veal, but first season it with the former spices and salt; put it in the Pie with some slices of veal under it, season them, and some also on the top, with some slices of lard and butter; close it up, and being baked, liquor it with clarified butter. Thus for to eat cold; if hot, liquor it with white-wine, gravy and butter.'
(Robert May, *The Accomplisht Cook Or the Art and Mystery of Cooking*)

V

Vesiga Filling

Vesiga is the spinal 'marrow' of the sturgeon and is little used except in Russian cooking. It comes to you in the form of a hard gelatinous band and requires five hours' soaking in cold water before being cooked (Preferably by steaming) until soft. Chop the vesiga and mix it with a few chopped hard-boiled eggs, some finely chopped onions which have been allowed to 'fall' in butter, and a little chopped parsley. Finally add sufficient well-reduced fish stock to bind the mixture and allow this to cool before use (normally used to stuff Piroschki).
(William Heptinstall)

W

Windsor Filling

100g cooked chicken chopped; 100g cooked ham shredded; 25g soft butter, 4-6 tablespoons mayonnaise; sprinkling of chopped parsley; squeeze of lemon; salt and pepper.

Mix butter and mayonnaise with other ingredients. Sufficient to fill 4-6 sandwiches.

(Elizabeth Kent, *Picnic Basket*)

X

X Marcel Boulestin's Beurre de Sardines

'Take one or two tins of sardines, carefully remove the skin and bones and pound in a mortar; add the same quantity of butter, a little salt and pepper and mix thoroughly so that it become a very smooth paste. You can, if you like, add to the mixture a few cooked soft roes. The mixture will keep for several days in an ice chest, but it should always be served very cold, the consistency being that of butter on a cold day. You can either give it a shape or keep it in a terrine. It is also delicious for sandwiches.'

(Recipes of Boulestin)

Y

York Ham

Jambon de York – York Ham, which is prepared in the town of the same name in England, has the reputation of being the best in Europe.
Yorkshire pigs are remarkable for their early maturity, but their fat is a little soft, and their meat is accompanied by a large proportion of fat.'

(Larousse Gastronomique)

Z

Zwetschgenpavesen

Cut 500g prunes in half and remove their stones. Bring 1 bottle full-bodied red wine to the boil with a stick of cinnamon, 4 cloves and 4 tablespoons sugar. Add the prunes and remove immediately from heat. Leave prunes to cool overnight.

Sandwich slices of white bread with a spoonful of the purée, dip sandwiches in egg-and-milk or a pancake batter, and fry them in butter until crisp and golden.

(Elizabeth Luard, *The Barricaded Larder*)

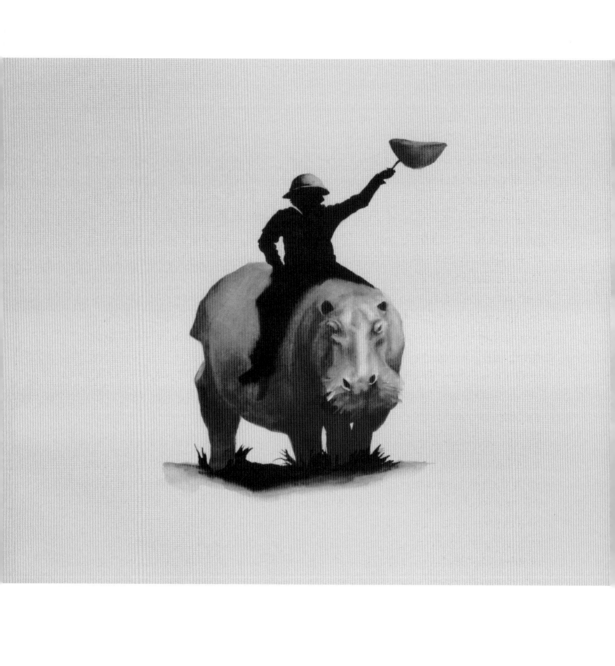

En Fin

I had set out in this book to cover stories of picnics and outdoor eating as comprehensively as I could but even with so long a list of wonderful and extraordinary sources and contributors, I admit defeat. With every book, new or old, I now pick up, another alfresco scene leaps from the pages with ambience, food and drink perfectly pictured and lusciously described, demanding my attention and inclusion amongst the others. What indeed to do? These picnics, however many they have become, were neither a vocation nor meant to become an everlasting occupation but only in the end a personal selection to share from the bottomless supply of remembered frippery picnic amusements occasionally spiced with more dramatic tales of life, death and adventure. Many of the stories were lost in their own time in the pages of the old books that have so appealed to me since childhood, many of the recipes too of course, especially those that appear so unappealing to contemporary tastes.

The food we eat indoors as well as out will change faster this century than ever before as science and climate change play a push-me-pull-you game with the problems and shortages of high population and radical weather. All our food may become freeze-dried like space food or sealed packets of extruded nuts and beans perfectly balanced for optimum nutrition like the extraordinary pulpy nut that now saves lives among malnourished children in the hungriest parts of the world, or, in the case of the rich and fat, to avoid obesity, as well as for cost and ease of distribution. Everything we eat may become a desiccated picnic with no cooking involved and an endless supply of pre-packed, identical vitamin balanced foods, prescribed and created in a laboratory with no scope for imagination, conversation or differing tastes.

Picnic Crumbs

It is an altogether depressing prospect when you think of the varieties of food and venues for its consumption that appear in so many different memories in a book describing only or mainly portable eating possibilities, even those that sound most unappetising. Until food really is only human fuel, I would rather, at the last, hope that this picnic of other people's picnics might be considered an *amuse guele* to an apparently unending menu of outdoor plans and provisions, picnic tales and tastes, at least for those not yet suffering terminal alfresco indigestion. I think all these bits and pieces of my own and other people's picnics, packed lunches and provisions have had that effect on me and at the very end I will leave the foie gras and lobster, even the sticky sausages and simple salads and settle for a perfectly simple egg sandwich for my last picnic, wherever and whenever that happens to be.

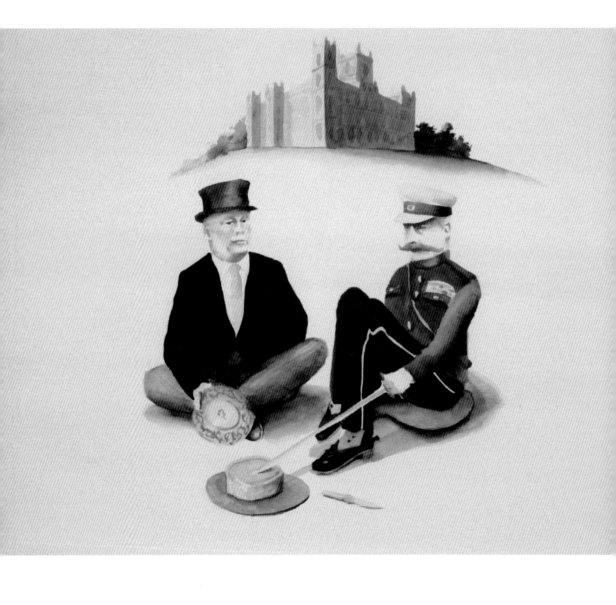

Bibliography

Anderson, Digby, *The Spectator Book of Imperative Cooking,* Harrap, London, 1987.

—— *The English At Table*, Social Affairs Unit 2006.

Army & Navy Stores, Catalogue, 1907.

Barbero, Alessandro, *The Battle, A New History of Waterloo*, translated from the Italian by John Cullen, Atlantic Books, London.

Beard, Nathaniel Thomas, *Some Recollections of Yesterday* published in the periodical *Temple Bar* 1894.

Bedford, Sybille, *A Visit to Don Otavio: A Traveller's Tale from Mexico,* 1953.

Beeton, Isabella, *Household Management,* Ward, Lock & Co., London, 1892.

Bird, Isabella, *Unbeaten Tracks in Japan, An Account of Travels in the Interior including Visits to the Aborigines of Yezo and the Shrine of Nikko,* John Murray, 1911.

Boorde, Andrew, *The Fyrst Boke of the Introduction of Knowledge,* 1870 (facsimile of 1547 edition).

Boulestin, X Marcel, *Recipes of Boulestin,* Heinemann, London, 1971.

Boxer, Arabella, *The Vogue Summer Cookbook,* Mitchell Beazley, London, 1980.

——, *The Vogue Winter Cookbook,* Mitchell Beazley, London, 1980.

Brennan, Jennifer, *Curries and Bugles,* Periplus Editions (HK) Ltd., Boston and Singapore, 2000.

Burton, David, *The Raj at Table,* Faber & Faber, London, 1993.

Capon, Robert Farrar, *The Romance of the Word: One Man's Love Affair with Theology,* Wm.B. Eerdmans Publishing Co., Grand Rapids, Michigan, 1995.

Case, Elizabeth; Wyman, Martha, Cook Away: *The Outing Cook Book.* Longmans, Green, NY, 1937.

Cheyne, George, *An Essay of Health and Long Life,* George Strahan and J. Leake, 1745.

Clark, Atwood, *Country Mix – Reminiscences of Rural Life and Sport in 19th Century England,* 1934 (Home Farm Books 2006).

Colchester-Wemyss, Sir Francis, *The Pleasures of the Table,* James Nisbet & Co Ltd, London, 1931.

Colquhoun, Kate, *Taste,* Bloomsbury, London, 2007, (quoting *The English Woman's Domestic Magazine,* edited by Samuel Beeton).

Cornwell, Bernard, *Sharpe's Waterloo,* Harper Collins, 1990.

Cowley Lambert, Isaac, *Trip to Cashmere and Ladak,* Henry S. King, London, 1877.

Creative Cooking and Entertaining, Readers Digest, London, 1986.

Dalgairns, Mrs, *The Practice of Cookery: Adapted to the Business of Every Day Life,* Robert Cadell, Edinburgh, 1830.

David, Elizabeth, *An Omelette and a Glass of Wine,* Penguin, Middlesex, 1984.

——, *English Bread and Yeast Cookery,* Book Club Associates, London, 1978.

——, *South Wind Through the Kitchen,* (Ed. Jill Norman) Michael Joseph, 1997.

——, *Spices, Salt and Aromatics in the English Kitchen,* Penguin, Middlesex, 1970.

——, *Summer Cooking,* Penguin, London, 1965.

——, *The True Emulsion,* The Spectator, August, 1962.

Davidson, Alan, *The Oxford Companion to Food,* 2nd edition, ed. Tom Jaine, OUP, 2006.

Bibliography

Del Bene, Terry Alan, *The Donner Party Cookbook: A Guide to Survival on the Hastings Cutoff,* Quality Books, USA, 2003.

Downey, Andrew (Ed.) *Cookery Recipes by Famous People for Returned British Prisoners of War Association Cookery Book,* Arthur Barker, London, 1950.

Durrell, Gerald, *Fillets of Plaice,* Viking, 1971.

Eden, Emily, *Up the Country: Scenes and Characteristics of Hindostan,* R. Bentley, 1867.

Eden, Frederic, *The Nile without a Dragoman,* H.S. King & Co., London, 1871.

Ehrman, John W., *Notes on Aromatic Sulphuric Acid and Confection of Senna,* The American Journal of Pharmacy, Vol. XLIII, 1871.

Esdaille, Charles, *The Peninsular War,* Allen Lane, London, 2002.

Farley, John, *The London Art of Cookery and Domestic Housekeeper's Complete Assistant,* 1787.

Field, Michael & Frances, *A Quintet of Cuisines,* Time-Life International, Netherlands, 1977.

Fiennes, Ralph, *Mind Over Matter,* Arrow, London, 1999.

Fisher, M.F.K., *The Gastronomical Me, An Alphabet for Gourmets, Serve it Forth, Consider the Oyster,* republished in *The Art of Cooking,* 50th Anniversary Edition, Wiley Publishing Inc, NY, 2004.

Fitzgibbon, Theodore, *The Pleasures of the Table,* OUP, Oxford, 1981, *Memorandum for the Guidance of Pursers and Stewards-in-Charge on Victualling and Management,* P & O Company, 1908.

Fleming, Peter, *One's Company: A Journey to China,* Cape, 1934.

Forster, E.M., *A Passage to India,* 1924.

Fraser, Flora, adapted *Diaries of Maud Berkeley,* Secker & Warburg, London, 1985.

Fuller, Thomas, *Pharmacopoeia Extemporanea,* London, 1710.

Ginsburg, Allen, *Reality Sandwiches,* City Lights Books, San Francisco, 1966.

Gordon, Constance Eveline, *The Anglo-Indian Cuisine,* A.J. Combridge and Co, Bombay, 1904.

Graham, G, *Life in the Mofussil: or, The Civilian in Lower Bengal,* C.K. Paul & Co, London, 1878.

Groden, Leo, *My Royal Cookbook,* typescript, 1962-1964.

Hall, Miranda, *Packed Lunches and Picnics,* Judy Piatkus Ltd., London, 1985.

Hanbury Tenison, Marika, *First Catch Your Crocodile,* published in *The Sunday Telegraph Cookbook,* Granada, London, 1980.

Hare, Ensign William, Photocopied typescript memoirs of Ensign William Henry Hare, 51st (2nd Yorkshire, West Riding) Regiment of Foot, 1868. Archives of National Army Museum.

Heptinstall, William, *Hors D'Oeuvre and Cold Table, A Book of Tried and Trusted Methods,* Faber & Faber Ltd. London, 1959.

Herzog, Maurice, *Annapurna,* Jonathan Cape, London, 1952.

Heyerdahl, Thor, *The Kon-Tiki Expedition,* Allen & Unwin, 1964.

Hillyard, Cdr. G.W., *Ideal Shipmate,* Memoir, (quoted in *King George V,* Kenneth Rose, Macmillan, London, 1983).

Hodgson Burnett, Frances, *A Little Princess,* 1905.

Houlston & Wright, *Enquire Within Upon Everything,* London, 1867.

Hull, Edmund C.P., *The European in India or, Anglo-Indian's Vade Mecum,* Henry S. King & Co, London, 1872.

Hume, Rosemary, *Party Food and Drink,* Chatto & Windus, London, 1950.

Jaffrey, Madhur, *A Taste of India,* Pavilion Books, London, 1983.

Jefferies, Richard, *The Life of the Fields,* London, 1893.

Jekyll, Agnes, *Kitchen Essays,* Thomas Nelson & Sons, London, 1922.

Jerome K Jerome, *Three Men in a Boat,* Arrowsmith, London, 1889.

Bibliography

Kennan, George, *Tent Life in Siberia,* 1870.

Kenney Herbert, Arthur Robert, *Culinary Jottings: A Treatise In Thirty Chapters on Reformed Cookery for Anglo-Indian Exiles,* Richardson & Co, 1885 (reprinted by Kessinger Publishing 2008).

Kent, Elizabeth, *Picnic Basket,* Fontana, Glasgow, 1978.

—— quoting the *Girl's Own Paper* in *Picnic Basket.*

Lapierre, Alexandra, *Women Travelers: A Century of Trailblazing Adventures 1850-1950,* Flammarion, Paris, 2007.

Lear, Edward, *The Owl and the Pussycat,* 1871.

Lewis, C C, *Culinary Notes for Sind,* 1943 (quoted in Jennifer Brennan, *Curries and Bugles*).

Leyel, Hilda; Hartley, Olga, *The Gentle Art of Cookery,* Keegan Paul, London, 2004.

Leyel, Mrs C F, *Picnics for Motorists,* George Routledge & Sons Ltd., London, 1936.

Lind, James, *A Treatise of the Scurvy,* A. Kincaid & A. Donaldson, Edinburgh, 1753

Livingstone, David & Charles, *Narrative of an Expedition to the Zambesi and its Tributaries 1858-1864,* John Murray, 1865 (reprinted, Duckworth, London, 2001).

Lo, Ken; Stewart, Katie, *Food for Lovers,* Paddington Press, London, 1977.

Lock, Ron and Quantrill, Peter, *Zulu Victory,* Greenhill Books, London, 2002.

Luard, Elizabeth, *The Barricaded Larder,* Bantam Press, London, 1988.

Major L, *Breakfasts, Luncheons and Ball Suppers,* Chapman & Hall, London, 1887. *The Pytchley Book of Refined Cookery and Bills of Fare.*

Martin, Brian P, *Tales of the Old Gamekeepers,* David & Charles, Newton Abbot, 1989.

May, Robert, *The Accomplisht Cook Or the Art and Mystery of Cooking,* 1660. IndyPublish.com edition, Boston, Mass., 2008.

McNeill, F. Marian, *The Scots Kitchen,* Blackie & Son, Edinburgh, 1929.

—— *The Camper's Kitchen,* Alexander Maclehose & Co, London, 1933.

Ménage, Gilles, *Dictionnaire du Etymologique de la Langue Françoise,* 1750.

Montagné, Prosper, *Larousse Gastronomique,* 1st English Translation, Paul Hamlyn, London, 1961.

Moryson, Fynes , *An Itinerary,* 1617.

Muir, Rory, *Salamanca 1812*, Yale University Press, New Haven & London, 2001.

Nansen, Fridtjof, *Through Siberia: The Land of the Future,* Heinemann, London, 1914.

National Army Museum, Collection of 164 letters, postcards and other documents relating to Capt Maurice Asprey, 1st Bn The Buffs (East Kent Regiment), 1914-1918.

—— Pte John Rose, 50th Regiment, letter to his parents dated Varna, 28th Aug 1854.

New York Times, 2nd May 1901.

Nicholson, Juliet, *The Perfect Summer,* John Murray, London, 2006.

Norwich, John Julius, *A Taste for Travel,* Alfred A. Knopf, London, 1987.

Oliver, Charles, *Dinner at Buckingham Palace,* Metro Publishing Ltd., 2001.

Parkinson, Sidney, *A Journal of a Voyage to the South Seas in HMS Endeavour,* Stanfield Parkinson, London, 1773.

Petrinovich, Lewis F., *The Cannibal Within,* Walter de Gruyter, New York, 2000.

Pettigrew, Jane, *The Picnic,* Pitkin Publishing, Andover, Hants., 2006.

Peyton, Mike, *An Average War: Eighth Army to Red Army,* Maypole Press, 2000.

Pullar, Phillippa, *Consuming Passions,* Penguin, London, 1970.

Queen Victoria, *More Leaves from a Journal of our life in the Highlands,* Webb & Bower, Exeter, 1980.

Bibliography

—— *Letters,* 28th June 1838, Ed Arthur Christopher Benson, London, 1908.

Reay, Barry, *Rural Englands,* Palgrave Macmillan, Basingstoke, 2004.

Roberts and Morgan-Grenville, *No Ordinary Tourist,* Milton Mill Publishing Ltd, Bridport, Dorset, 2006.

Roberts, Kenneth, *The Gourmet Cookbook,* Gourmet Distributing Company, NY, 1950.

Roden, Claudia, *Picnics and Other Outdoor Feasts,* Grub Street, London, 2001.

Rome *News-Tribune,* May 20th, 1953.

Rose, Kenneth, *King George V* (to Sir Owen Morshead), Macmillan, London, 1983.

Sahib, Chota, *Camp Recipes for Camp People,* Madras, 1890.

Sampson Lowe Marston Searle & Rivington, *Sleepy Sketches; Or How We Live, And How We Do Not Live,* London 1877.

Schwabe, Calvin W., *Veterinary Epidemiologist,* University of Viriginia, Reprint, 1995.

Simpson, Helen, *The Cold Table,* Jonathan Cape, London, 1935.

Singh, Manju Shivraj, *A Taste of Palace Life, Royal Indian Cookery,* Windward, Leicester, 1987

Sitwell, Osbert, *Sing High! Sing Low!,* Macmillan & Co, London, 1944

Smollett, Tobias, *Travels through France and Italy,* 1766.

Smurthwaite, David, *A Recipe for Discontent,* National Army Museum archive.

Solomon, Charmaine, *The Complete Asian Cookbook,* Paul Hamlyn, 1976.

Solum, Lyla G, *For Danish Appetites,* Danish Village Gifts, Solvang, California, 1955.

Soyer, Alexis, *The Pantropheon,* Simpkin, Marshall & Co., London, 1853.

—— *The Selected Soyer,* (Ed. Andrew Langley), Absolute Press, Bath, 1987.

Spry, Constance, *The Constance Spry Cookery Book,* J. M. Dent & Co, 1964.

St Clair, Lady Harriett, *Dainty Dishes,* J. B. Lippincott & Co. 1866.

Stanley, Louis T., *The London Season,* Hutchinson, London, 1955.

Strathern, Paul, *Napoleon in Egypt,* Bantam, London, 2008.

Surtees, R.S., *Plain or Ringlets,* Bradbury, Agnew & Co, 1883.

Tannahill, Reay, *Food in History,* Penguin, Revised Edition, London, 1988.

The Cooking of Russia, Time-Life International, Nederland, N.V., 1971.

Theroux, Paul, *The Great Railway Bazaar,* Penguin, 1977.

Thesiger, Wilfred, *Arabian Sands,* 1959.

Thornton, James, *Your Most Obedient Servant,* Webb & Bower, Exeter, 1985.

Trollope, Anthony, *He Knew He Was Right,* 1869.

Walton, Izaak, *The Compleat Angler,* 1653.

Ward, Geoffrey, *Before the Trumpet: Young Franklin Roosevelt, 1882-1905,* Harper and Row, NY, 1985.

Washington, Mrs, *The Unrivalled Cook and Housekeepers Guide,* Harper & Bros., NY, 1885.

Watson, Alfred Edward Thomas, *English Sport,* Macmillan and Co., NY 1903 (originally from Badminton Magazine, *Racecourse and Covert Side,* 1883).

Weir, Robin; Liddell, Caroline & Brears, Peter C.D., *Recipes from the Dairy,* National Trust, London, 1998.

Westminster, Loelia, Duchess of, *Grace & Favour,* Weidenfeld & Nicholson, London, 1961.

White, Florence, *Good Things in England,* 1931, re-published Persephone Books, London, 1999.

Wiltshire Federation of Women's Institutes, *Wiltshire, Within Living Memory,* WFWI Devizes & Countryside Books, Newbury, 1993.

Bibliography

Wodehouse, P G, *Jeeves and the Old School Chum,* quoted in Kent, Elizabeth, *Picnic Basket,* Fontana, London, 1978.

Woodward, Sarah, *Moorish Food,* Kyle Cathie Ltd., London, 1998 .

Wooler, Neil, *Dinner in the Diner: The History of Railway Catering,* David & Charles, 1987.

Young, Donald (Ed.), *The Search for the Source of the Nile,* Correspondence between Captain Richard Burton and Captain John Speke, The Roxburghe Club, London, 1999.